Five Things Every Christian ~~Should~~ **Must** Know

by

Floyd Bland

© 2018 by Floyd W. Bland. All rights reserved. No portion of this book may be reproduced without permission, except as permitted by U.S. copyright law. For permissions, please contact: info@notwm.org

The views expressed in this book are those of the author and are intended for Christian inspirational purposes only. Every effort has been made to ensure its content is insightful for Christian living at press time.

This book is not written to be an exhaustive treatment of its content, and no liability is assumed for losses or damages from the information provided. Also, it is not written to provide legal or clinical advice. If clinical or legal advice is needed, the services of a competent professional should be sought. The reader is advised to take full responsibility for their personal safety and well-being.

Some content has been recreated from events, locales, and conversations from the author's memory. Unless otherwise stated, all details have been altered to maintain anonymity. Any resemblance to actual persons living or dead, organizations, events, or locales is purely coincidental.

Unless otherwise noted, all Scripture quotations are taken from the New King James Version®. Copyright © 1982 by Thomas Nelson. Used by permission. All rights reserved.

Scripture quotations marked (NLT) are taken from the Holy Bible, New Living Translation, copyright ©1996, 2004, 2015 by Tyndale House Foundation. Used by permission of Tyndale House Publishers, Inc., Carol Stream, Illinois 60188. All rights reserved.

Some images used for chapter headings are officially licensed from ©Graphics Factory.com.

ISBN-13: 978-0-9909823-8-8

Jesus Christ is Lord!

Contents

With Gratitude: viii

Introduction: Yearning for More   1
- *A Private Meeting* • *My Private Meeting* • *Five Important Things*

Chapter 1: In Christ, We Are Forgiven   21
- *Son of God and Son of Man* • *The Forgiveness of Sin* • *Freedom in Christ* • *Peace with God*

Chapter 2: In Christ, We Have Ultimate Assurance   38
- *A Fleeting Allusion* • *We have Security* • *Faithful and Enduring Promises* • *God Sustains Us*

Chapter 3: In Christ, We Have Purpose and Identity   52
- *Fearfully and Wonderfully Created* • *God's Purpose and Grace* • *More Than Conquerors*

Chapter 4: In Christ, We Have Eternal Fellowship   72
- *One in Christ* • *Communion with God*

Chapter 5: In Christ, We Are New Creations   92
- *A New Perspective* • *A New Lifestyle* • *Making a Difference*

About the Author   112

With Gratitude

I am grateful to God for sending His Son to die for my sins, to raise Him for my justification, and for His Spirit who is the security deposit for my glorious, eternal home He has prepared for all those who love His appearing (2 Timothy 4:8).

I am grateful for my parents whose love, faith, and piety inspire me to live for Christ even today. For my loving and supporting wife and family, I will always thank God for you.

To those many unassuming, unsung heroes and heroines who make up my extended family, I thank God for your prayers, encouragement, and assistance that helped to make this book possible.

Finally to Paramita Bhattacharjee of *Creative Paramita* and Pam Lagomarsino of *Above The Pages Editorial Services*. Thank God for your cover graphics and final edits to help prepare this book for its publication.

Introduction
Yearning for More

A Private Meeting

The moon must have been especially bright on the  evening when Nicodemus met Jesus privately, as John records in the third chapter of his gospel. A distinguished community member, Nicodemus was a Pharisee and a Sanhedrin member.

The Pharisees differed from the Sadducees and the Scribes — the two other major religious sects at that time. Not only were they the largest and most influential, but they were also recognized as the ceremonial purists and religious traditionalists for God's chosen people, Israel and "the true and loyal standard-bearers of traditional Israel."[1]

The Sanhedrin served as the supreme Jewish authority. It consisted of esteemed Jewish leaders from all three major religious sects, a priest, and a presiding high priest. Much like the three branches of our government in the US capital today, this assembly provided governance for all public matters both civil and religious.[2]

Sacred Scripture is silent regarding the meeting's exact time and place except where John tells us it happened during *Passover*, which is a major Jewish observance that runs concurrently with the *Feast of*

Unleavened Bread (from the fourteenth day through the twenty-first day of the first month of the Jewish calendar or *Nisan*[3]).

During this week of feasting and celebration, massive throngs of people flooded Jerusalem from all over the world as these scholars attest:

> The number of permanent residents in the Jerusalem that Jesus knew was about six hundred thousand. A conservative estimate of the vast multitude of Passover pilgrims is about two million, who swelled the city's population to almost four times its normal size.[4]

Every Jewish male was required to attend this observance, which commemorates Israel's *Exodus* from over four hundred years of Egyptian slavery (see: Exodus 12:1–13:16, 23:17; 34:23).[5]

Yet with all the festive merry-making, Nicodemus was deeply troubled. He yearned for an opportunity to meet Jesus Christ so he could talk privately—*and listen*. Something intrigued him about the Lord. Perhaps it was His many miracles, or maybe it was His remarkable teachings about the *Kingdom of God* that somehow resonated within his heart.

It could have been the stories from people whose lives had been changed completely after they met Jesus that fascinated him. Ultimately, there was something about Jesus both captivating and disturbing to Nicodemus, as one author notes:

> [Nicodemus] recognized in Jesus something he had never yet encountered. He was so impressed that he sought a private interview with this new teacher, and arranged an appointment with Jesus "by night." The fact that Nicodemus came to Jesus by night certainly is no evidence of cowardice on his part. It was the natural thing to do.[6]

One can only imagine what must have gone through his mind as he made his way through the streets of Jerusalem with its multitudes of festive revelers, musicians, and celebrators to a secluded place where he could spend time with the Lord one-on-one.

Although this meeting was outside the norm since both the Pharisees and the Sanhedrin opposed Jesus, Nicodemus saw it as crucial. Ultimately, it would help him find the answer to the age-old question many of his contemporaries were asking: "Is this teacher our long-awaited *Messiah*?"

John records the meeting in John 3:1–21:

> [1]There was a man of the Pharisees named Nicodemus, a ruler of the Jews. [2]This man came to Jesus by night and said to Him, "Rabbi, we know that You are a teacher

come from God; for no one can do these signs that You do unless God is with him."

³ Jesus answered and said to him, "Most assuredly, I say to you, unless one is born again, he cannot see the kingdom of God." ⁴ Nicodemus said to Him, "How can a man be born when he is old? Can he enter a second time into his mother's womb and be born?"

⁵ Jesus answered, "Most assuredly, I say to you, unless one is born of water and the Spirit, he cannot enter the kingdom of God. ⁶ That which is born of the flesh is flesh, and that which is born of the Spirit is spirit. ⁷ Do not marvel that I said to you, 'You must be born again.' ⁸ The wind blows where it wishes, and you hear the sound of it, but cannot tell where it comes from and where it goes. So is everyone who is born of the Spirit."

⁹ Nicodemus answered and said to Him, "How can these things be?"

¹⁰ Jesus answered and said to him, "Are you the teacher of Israel, and do not know these things? ¹¹ Most assuredly, I say to you, We speak what We know and testify what We have seen, and you do not receive Our witness.

¹² If I have told you earthly things and you do not believe, how will you believe if I tell you heavenly things? ¹³ No one has ascended to heaven but He who came

down from heaven, that is, the Son of Man who is in heaven.

[14] And as Moses lifted up the serpent in the wilderness, even so must the Son of Man be lifted up, [15] that whoever believes in Him should not perish but have eternal life.

[16] For God so loved the world that He gave His only begotten Son, that whoever believes in Him should not perish but have everlasting life. [17] For God did not send His Son into the world to condemn the world, but that the world through Him might be saved.

[18] "He who believes in Him is not condemned; but he who does not believe is condemned already, because he has not believed in the name of the only begotten Son of God.

[19] And this is the condemnation, that the light has come into the world, and men loved darkness rather than light, because their deeds were evil. [20] For everyone practicing evil hates the light and does not come to the light, lest his deeds should be exposed. [21] But he who does the truth comes to the light, that his deeds may be clearly seen, that they have been done in God."

Such passages in the gospel of John have always resonated with me. John is known for featuring various aspects of the *Deity of Christ* using easily understood imagery. John's gospel differs vastly from the *Synoptic Gospels*, which parallel Jesus' life from different perspectives.

For instance, Matthew's gospel shows how Christ fulfills Old Testament prophesies as the promised *Messiah* (to appeal to a Jewish audience); Mark's gospel presents the Lord's active ministry of mighty acts and miracles, while Luke's gospel emphasizes the Lord's humanity as the *Son of Man*.

Within this narrative, John shows how it is by the *Son of God* we can have an eternal, personal fellowship with God. It contains the foundational New Testament passages that illustrate: a) God's selfless love in action, b) how Jesus Christ secures our eternal favor with God, and c) how faith in Jesus grants us God's gift of eternal life.

The meeting begins with Nicodemus greeting the Lord as the "Rabbi" (Teacher) who has been sent by God (v. 2). But Jesus was not concerned about receiving accolades; He was more concerned with the eternal destiny of His esteemed visitor and responds by stressing the need to be *Born Again* to see the *Kingdom of God* (v. 3).

Nicodemus did not understand the spiritual implications of what Jesus was saying, and he associates it with normal childbirth by asking how it was possible to re-enter the womb as an adult (v. 4). Here, one writer notes:

> Nicodemus had failed utterly to grasp the idea of the spiritual birth as essential to entrance into the Kingdom of God. He knew only Jews as members of that kingdom, the political kingdom of Pharisaic hope which was to make all the world Jewish (Pharisaic) under the King Messiah.[7]

Some say rightly that the distance between Heaven and Hell is approximately twelve to eighteen inches—*the distance between the head and the heart.* So to clearly communicate this fundamental yet essential spiritual truth, the Lord appeals to the human heart by telling a most wonderful story about God, our loving Father; Jesus Christ, the One and only Son of God, and the world, or all humanity.

In verse 5, the Lord uses childbirth metaphors to show the difference between the normal (water) birth with embryonic fluid, and the second (spiritual) birth that the Spirit of God performs.

Then the Lord refers to a simple law of reproduction: flesh can only produce flesh, and the Spirit will only produce spirit (v. 6). Normal childbirth cannot produce a spiritually transformed life. It will only reproduce more of itself—*flesh.* Likewise, the Spirit of God will not produce sinful human beings because this would be inconsistent with His holy nature.

There must be a dynamic, spiritual transformation inside us before we can see the *Kingdom of God*. This is because we are spiritually broken due to *Original Sin*, the internal condition that produces outward signs of moral depravity. It happened after our ancestors, Adam and Eve, disobeyed God in the Garden of Eden. As a result, we are born without a love for God or godly things, and we choose to disobey Him, just as they did (see: Genesis 2:16–17, 3, Romans 5:12).

Concerning our wretched internal condition or *Natural Man*, one scholar comments:

> [The Natural Man] will make no effort to remove his moral corruption, for he does not desire its removal. He is satisfied with the state of his heart, and lives according to its inclinations. He is the voluntary slave to sin, and is therefore pleased with the slavery.[8]

Some think that *Fallen Nature*, sin, and moral depravity are all outdated ideas, and we do not need God's intervention. When asked about salvation, they reply: "Me, a sinner? Impossible! I have the 'right' name, and I have all the 'right' connections. Besides, I have all the 'right' things this world can offer. *I don't need anything!*"

There is a real danger here when our pride and self-righteousness fools us into a false sense of self-security. We think God accepts us and we will make it to Heaven because we say and do all the "right things."

But unless our "right things" are the byproducts of our spiritual change, we will continue to miss the mark even on our best day. King David observes in Psalm 51:5 that we were all born in sin and shaped in iniquity. He also states in Psalm 14:2–3:

> The Lord looks down from heaven upon the children of men, To see if there are any who understand, who seek God. They have all turned aside, They have together become corrupt; There is none who does good, No, not one.

It is this nature that makes us think, speak, and act—often without provocation—in ways detrimental to others and us that we *need to change.*

The good news is God can change our governing disposition from vile and sinful to pure and holy, through the *Born Again* experience (*Regeneration*) as this theologian observes: "Regeneration is that act of God by which the governing disposition of the soul is made holy…It is God turning the soul to Himself."[9]

A computer contaminated by a virus can still function, but not at its optimum level. However, once the virus is removed, the hard drive is reformatted with new software installed; the machine can function at an optimum level according to its original design. Much like this computer illustration, sin contaminated us, and we need spiritual reformatting.

Here, we acknowledge our contamination by confessing our sin before God. Then we turn from the continual practice of sinful behavior through repentance. We place our faith in the Lord Jesus Christ, who installs the spirit-directed software, which enables us to function according to our original design—*at full capacity*!

As 2 Corinthians 5:17 tells us, we are totally "new creatures." Now, loving and pleasing God is our new all-consuming, lifelong objective. No longer do we seek the things of the world. They have become dead to us, and we are no longer subject to them. Our new aim is to live lives that emulate our Lord and live for Him to the best of our ability for the rest of our lives.

We were once proud and selfish; now humble and selfless, once aggressive and villainous; now assertive and virtuous. In place of deceit, we now practice sincerity. Once we sought to victimize others through hypocrisy, betrayal, and lies. Now we interact with God, others, and ourselves with authenticity, faithfulness, and truth at all levels. Our spiritual transformation is all-encompassing as the Holy Spirit, who now dwells within us, enables us to perform the perfect will of God on the outside.

Next, Jesus uses a wind analogy to describe our spiritual transformation. Although we can see and feel its effects, the wind is naked to the human eye (v. 8).

God's *Omnipotent* Holy Spirit has been changing the lives of people (including ours) for over six thousand years of human history. His refining work can be as subtle as a soft, gentle breeze or as dramatic as a devastating tornado.

Jesus Christ is the only solution to our spiritual quandary. To illustrate this point, He states that as the Son of Man, He came down from Heaven to reveal God's plan of redemption fully (v. 13).

He recounts the story when the children of Israel sinned in the wilderness, as recorded in Numbers 21:4–9. Fiery serpents were sent to bite those who rebelled against Moses and God — many died. The people cried to Moses asking for forgiveness. To alleviate their suffering, the Lord instructed Moses to make a brass, fiery serpent and attach it to a pole. Dying people who looked at the brass serpent were miraculously healed instantly.

Jesus said He likewise would be "lifted up," and whoever believes in Him will have eternal life. He also tells Nicodemus that His death is motivated by God's love and not to condemn us, but to heal our spiritual condition forever (vs. 15–17).

Faith is instrumental in becoming righteous before God, and our condemnation is not based on our sinful acts, but our rejection of His redemptive work performed on the cross (v.18).

These teachings on faith and righteousness are consistent with two well-known Old Testament Scriptures:

> And [Abraham] believed the LORD, and the LORD counted him as righteous because of his faith (Genesis 15:6 NLT).

> Behold the proud, His soul is not upright in him; But the just shall live by his faith (Habakkuk 2:4).

As the meeting closes, the Lord affirms His deity as the Light (of the World)[10] and says some will choose to remain in darkness because of their unbelief and love for darkness and its sin. Then He assures Nicodemus (and us) that whoever lives by the truth comes into the light (Jesus), and all we do is done in God's sight (vs. 19–21).

It is worth noting Nicodemus understood Jesus, and his life was changed. This became evident later, during the Feast of Tabernacles (or Booths), when Jesus proclaimed these words to the crowds assembled at Jerusalem:

> Anyone who is thirsty may come to me! Anyone who believes in me may come

and drink! For the Scriptures declare, 'Rivers of living water will flow from his heart' (John 7:37b–38 NLT).

When Jesus was condemned for what He said, it was Nicodemus who spoke up on His behalf (John 7:50). Also after the crucifixion, when all His disciples had either betrayed or forsaken Him, again it was Nicodemus, along with Joseph of Arimathea who went to Pilate—the local Roman magistrate—to obtain the body. Then they wrapped Jesus' body in cloths using the spices he purchased and laid Him in Joseph's tomb (John 19:38-42).

We may never know the full extent of Nicodemus' transformation. But we know Jesus answered his questions.

My Private Meeting

I can recall the time in my life when I yearned for a personal meeting with Jesus. Like Nicodemus, I too was intrigued by the Lord after reading and learning about Him from the gospel accounts.

The more I read and learned about His life and ministry, the more enamored with Him I became. Then as I took an honest look at my level of spiritual understanding and commitment and compared them to the Lord's and to his first-century followers, I became more dissatisfied with my level of spiritual development.

I could identify with the psalmist: "As the deer longs for streams of water, so I long for you, O God. I thirst for God, the living God (Psalm 42:1–2 NLT)." I longed for a deeper fellowship with the Lord so that I could learn more about Him and do more for Him. In other words, I "hungered and thirsted" for His righteousness (Matthew 5:6), and wanted it to permeate every fiber of my being.

I wanted to know more about His love and forgiveness; His *grace* and mercy; His power over sin and self; His *Providence,* and His perfect will for me as this definition infers:

> [Providence is] God's purpose and plan for the universe and the carrying out of them by His almighty power and holy love. This includes the certainty of the triumph of God's purpose at the end of the age and His use now...of human intentions and activities in history. God's ultimate purpose centers in Jesus Christ, and God's ways cannot be understood apart from Him (John 1:3; Hebrews 1:1). God acts in human history secretly and mysteriously for the good of His elect people, using the free decisions and sinful activities of men for his own ends (Romans 8:28).[11]

I wanted to know more about where He wanted me to go and what He wanted me to do, although

I was actively serving within my church and community. I had a very strong sense I could surrender more of my life to the Lord in a way that escaped me at that time. Then after praying, fasting, and seeking guidance from my parents, Christian mentors, and pastors, the Lord sent me nearly 500 miles away from home and all that was familiar to me—away from distractions—to seek Him. It was a difficult transition at first. But as time passed, the Lord revealed my need for greater surrender and service.

Let me say there was nothing wrong with the life I left behind or the people in it. The Lord used it and them to spark a desire in me for Him that would change my life forever. But I must also confess that my life would not have changed in the way it has had I stayed where I was.

My "meeting" happened on Wednesday evening, November 2, 1977; the moon seemed especially bright on that evening. But unlike Nicodemus, the meeting did not result in a *Born Again* experience for me since I had accepted Jesus Christ as my personal Lord and Savior many years before. Instead, it resulted in my clearly hearing God's gentle "call" on my life for the ministry. For unbeknownst to me, I had been "running" from the Lord for about seven years; this night, I stopped running—and surrendered.

Although my family, pastor, church family, and friends were not surprised when I formally announced my "call," they were very pleased and supportive regarding it. My "trial sermon" was on Sunday, December 11, 1977, and I became an ordained minister a few years later. Over time, the Lord allowed me to become a husband and father, ministry administrator, chaplain, and to serve in local churches as an associate and interim pastor.

I must confess the "yearning" has not waned over the years. But I have learned it can be extremely dangerous to the human psyche. It requires our willingness to empty ourselves of all pride and self-interest so we can reach a level of total vulnerability, humility, and dependence on Jesus Christ alone.

But there is also some great news here. When we willingly surrender our all to the Lord, then He can perform His best and most wonderful work in us just as Philippians 1:6 teaches:

> Being confident of this very thing, that He who has begun a good work in you will complete it until the day of Jesus Christ.

Five Important Things

Over the years, I have learned every Christian must know five things:

1. In Christ, we are forgiven.
2. In Christ, we have ultimate assurance.
3. In Christ, we have purpose and identity.

4. In Christ, we have eternal fellowship.
5. In Christ, we are new creations.

I wrote this book to stimulate a greater longing for the things of God through a personal encounter with Jesus Christ. The book will feature important Bible passages and the works of other authors. I have highlighted theological terms in *italics* to aid in further research as needed.

While we await His glorious return, let us take comfort in how God's Word, the Bible, defines us and not how the world defines us. Then, we can capture and celebrate these five essential, spiritual characteristics. *What about you?*

Before presenting Chapter 1, I will share a classic hymn that shows one person's yearning for a personal encounter with the Lord.

It's Real[12]
Homer L. Cox

> Oh, how well do I remember how I doubted day by day, For I did not know for certain that my sins were washed away; When the Spirit tried to tell me, I would not the truth receive, I endeavored to be happy, and to make myself believe.

> When the truth came close and searching, all my joy would disappear, For I did not have the witness of the Spirit bright and

clear; If at times the coming judgment would appear before my mind, Oh, it made me so uneasy, for God's smile I could not find.

When the Lord sent faithful servants who would dare to preach the truth, How my heart did so condemn me as the Spirit gave reproof; Satan said at once, 'Twill ruin you to now confess your state; Keep on working and professing, and you'll enter heaven's gate."

So I prayed to God in earnest, and not caring what folks said, I was hungry for the blessing; my poor soul, it must be fed; Then at last by faith I touched Him, and, like sparks from smitten steel, Just so quick salvation reached me, oh, bless God, I know it's real.

Refrain:
But it's real, (it's real), it's real, Oh, I know (I know), it's real; Praise God, the doubts are settled, For I know, I know it's real.
A-men.

Notes

[1] Dana, H. E. Dana. *The New Testament World*, revised 3rd ed., (Nashville: Broadman, 1937) 118.

[2] Dana, 115.

[3] The original name: *Abib* (Exodus 13:4) was changed to *Nisan* after Israel's *exile* from Babylonian captivity (see: Nehemiah 2:1, Esther 3:7).

[4] Rosen, Ceil and Moishe. *Christ in the Passover: Why is this Night Different*, 6th ed., (Chicago: Moody, 1980) 42.

[5] The mandatory feasts: *Passover/Unleavened Bread*, occur between our March and April, the *Feast of Weeks* or *Pentecost* occurs between May and June, and the *Feast of Booths* or *Tabernacles* occurs between September and October.

[6] Hester, H.I. *The Heart of the New Testament*, 35th ed., (Nashville: Broadman, 1981) 129.

[7] Robertson, Archibald Thomas. "Gospel of John," *Word Pictures in the New Testament*, reprint, vol. 4, (Grand Rapids: Baker, 1960) 45.

[8] Pendleton, James Madison. *Christian Doctrines, a Compendium of Theology*, 33rd ed., (Valley Forge: Judson, 1976) 183–184.

[9] Strong, Augustus H., *Systematic Theology*, 31st ed., (Valley Forge: Judson, 1976) 809.

[10] See: John 1:1–14; 8:12; 9:5; 12:46.

[11] Douglas. J.D. et al., "Providence," *The Concise Dictionary of the Christian Tradition: Doctrine, Liturgy, History*, (Grand Rapids: Regency, 1989) 309.

[12] Cox, Homer L. "It's Real," *The Baptist Standard Hymnal with Responsive Readings*, ed. Mrs. A. M. Townsend, (Nashville: Townsend, 1961) 271–72.

Chapter One

Chapter 1
In Christ, We Are Forgiven

Son of God and Son of Man

As it still does today, the idea that Jesus Christ is  the Son of God raised a few eyebrows in Jesus' day. On two separate occasions, those who heard His claims of deity tried to enact a sentence of capital punishment against Him, as Leviticus 24:16 authorized.

The first occasion happened while Jesus was at the Jerusalem Temple. There He told the Jewish leaders that Abraham rejoiced to see His day and that "Before Abraham was, I AM" (see: John 8:56-58).

Angered Jews tried to stone Jesus because they interpreted His words as blasphemy. Jesus escaped but found Himself in a similar situation on another visit to the temple when He declares:

> My sheep listen to My voice; I know them, and they follow me. I give them eternal life, and they will never perish. No one can snatch them away from me, for my Father has given them to me, and He is more powerful than anyone else. No one can snatch them from the Father's hand.

The Father and I are one (John 10:27–30 NLT).

Again, the mob sought to kill Him because He claimed to be God in human flesh (John 10:33). To them, He was establishing an unauthorized correlation between Himself and the Old Testament Covenant God (YHWH) (see: Exodus 3:13–15, 6:2–8).[1] One scholar makes this observation about why the Lord's claims of deity offended so many:

> In view of the fact that the Jehovah [YHWH] of the Jewish Old Testament would not give His name, honor, or glory to another, it is little wonder that the words and deeds of Jesus of Nazareth drew stones and cries of "blasphemy" from the first-century Jews. The very things that the Jehovah of the Old Testament claimed for Himself Jesus of Nazareth also claimed.[2]

Acknowledging Jesus Christ is the *Son of Man* is not much of a stretch because we have the benefit of historical records of His life and ministry that verify His existence. From these records, we know He walked the earth for about thirty-three years and had the same wants, needs, and desires all human beings have.

For instance, like any human, He experienced hunger, thirst, grief, fatigue, sorrow, happiness, and loneliness. He also had aspirations, expressed feelings of love and anger; and He slept, ate, drank, wept, and was tempted.

But, despite the many temptations He faced, He did not succumb to them. Nor did He yield to the lusts of the flesh, the eyes, and pride of life (1 John 2:16) or accommodate His self-centered agenda. Instead, He lived a completely balanced life of moral and spiritual excellence at all times. Unlike the rest of us, Jesus submitted Himself to the will of His Father and satisfied all the requirements of God's Law; He was perfect.

Understanding Jesus as Son of God becomes less of a problem when we acknowledge His being perfect as the Son of Man, and that perfection is an attribute of deity. When we understand Jesus as being 100 percent God in human flesh, all the components of His life and ministry makes perfect sense.

For instance, the Son of God correlates with Him demonstrating an imposing mastery over His creation. He commanded the storm to be silent and walked on the sea. He also turned water into wine, fed the multitudes, healed the sick, and raised the dead. These actions verified His claims to be God in human flesh.

John begins his book by declaring Jesus' deity as the Word in John 1:1: "And the Word [Jesus] was God." This verse lays the groundwork for the real possibility of our eternal God dwelling in human flesh as stated in John 1:14 (NLT):

> So the Word became human and made His home among us. He was full of unfailing love and faithfulness. And we have seen His glory, the glory of the Father's one and only Son.

It is humanly impossible to understand and explain the mysteries of God including the intricacies of His *Incarnation*. God has the authority to conceal or disclose anything He so chooses (Proverbs 25:2). Yet He revealed His divine, redemptive plan through Jesus Christ, the only Son of God. All that God requires is our faith in Christ to receive His gracious gift.

We can also acknowledge Christ as Savior because God promised to save all those who turned to Him according to Isaiah 45:22 (NLT): "Let all the world look to me for salvation! For I am God; there is no other."

It is worth noting the Old Testament portrays God as the only One who will judge the world in righteousness as Psalm 96:13 reads:

> For He is coming, for He is coming to judge the earth. He shall judge the world with righteousness, And the peoples with His truth.

In the New Testament, Jesus Christ is identified as the one God has bestowed all judgment as John 5:22–23 attests:

> For the Father judges no one, but has committed all judgment to the Son, that all should honor the Son just as they honor the Father. He who does not honor the Son does not honor the Father who sent Him.

As the righteous judge of the universe, only Jesus Christ is responsible for the forgiveness of sin.

The Forgiveness of Sin

The Bible teaches the payment for sin is death (Romans 6:23). Thus, someone has to die and shed blood to remediate sin as God states in Leviticus 17:11:

> For the life of the flesh is in the blood, and I have given it to you upon the altar to make atonement for your souls; for it is the blood that makes atonement for the soul.

Here, God was giving Moses specific instructions on how to erect an altar and use animal blood to pay for our sin (*Atonement*). God never intended for these rituals to solve our sin problem since they had to be repeated.

Instead, they foreshadowed a permanent, more efficacious restitution that would:

a) completely wash away our sins,
b) make us righteous before God, and
c) restore our lost, eternal fellowship with God.

A wonderful illustration of our redemption is presented in the *Suffering Servant* found in Isaiah 53:4–6:

> Surely He has borne our griefs and carried our sorrows; Yet we esteemed Him stricken, Smitten by God, and afflicted. But He was wounded for our transgressions, He was bruised for our iniquities; The chastisement for our peace was upon Him, And by His stripes we are healed. All we like sheep have gone astray; We have turned, every one, to his own way; And the LORD has laid on Him the iniquity of us all.

Matthew Chapter 9 tells the story of a paralyzed man whose friends brought him to Jesus for healing. Jesus makes this statement in verse 2 (NLT): "Be encouraged, my child! Your sins are forgiven." Then He makes this declaration in verse 6 (NLT): "'So I will prove to you that the Son of Man has the authority on earth to forgive sins.' Then Jesus turned to the paralyzed man and said, 'Stand up, pick up your mat, and go home.'"

Until this time, no human being had been authorized to forgive sin. Only God forgave sin. Yet, Jesus now insists that He forgives all our sin—past, present, and future. He claimed this because He was the One who would satisfy all the statutes of the *Old Testament Law*, and He would offer Himself as the perfect sacrifice for our sin.

Jesus Christ fulfills three roles for our benefit. He is the *Prophet*, whose life and teaching give us moral and spiritual direction as foretold by Moses in Deuteronomy 18:15–22.

The Bible, which contains His teaching is our perfect guide to living in the *New Testament Age*. As we read, study, memorize, and apply its principles to our lives, we grow into His productive people of faith and grace.

Jesus is our *King*, who governs our hearts and minds through His Holy Spirit (and His Word). We love Him, willingly surrender to Him, and faithfully serve His church and those He describes as the "least of these" (Matthew 25:34–40). He is our *Sovereign Lord*, and we are subjects of His eternal *Kingdom*. He is the focal point of our love and gratitude as well as the "author and finisher" of our faith (Hebrews 12:2).

But, He is our *Great High Priest*, in whom we have the forgiveness of sin. Hebrews 9:11–12 teaches He redeemed us by paying sin's price Himself:

> But Christ came as High Priest of the good things to come…Not with the blood of goats and calves, but with His own blood He entered the Most Holy Place once for all, having obtained eternal redemption.

Jesus' sacrificial death covers sin because He is the *Lamb of God* who takes away the sins of the world (John 1:29). By fulfilling these attributes, He is fully capable of saving "to the uttermost" all those who come to God by Him, seeing He lives forever to make intercession for us (Hebrews 7:25).

Freedom in Christ and peace with God are the two benefits of our forgiveness of sin.

Freedom in Christ

Whenever the word "freedom" is spoken, it conjures ideas of unlimited activity without external hindrance or restraint. This freedom yields some pleasure for a season, but it is never lasting or redemptive.

Let me pause here to say the precious civic freedoms we often take for granted in the US today were never intended to be our license to "do what we want when we want."

Instead, our civic freedom means having the sacred responsibility to act in the best interest of our civic good. That's why I am grateful for laws that guard against the anarchy and civic disorder that would ensue if our freedom as individuals were taken to their extreme.

The Bible teaches a level of eternal, redemptive freedom is available to us through Christ. In John 8:34–36 (NLT), the Lord conveys a message of this far greater freedom (my emphasis):

> Jesus answered them, "Most assuredly, I say to you, whoever commits sin is a slave of sin. And a slave does not abide in the house forever, but a son abides forever. Therefore if the Son makes you free, *you shall be free indeed.*

Although no one is standing over us like a slave master causing us to sin, one's sinful lifestyle can reveal one's true "master." Galatians 5:19–21 (NLT), presents a list of the despicable tasks (*Lusts of the Flesh*) we can perform for our "master" including "sexual immorality, impurity, lustful pleasures, idolatry, sorcery, hostility, quarreling, jealousy, outbursts of anger, selfish ambition, dissension, division, envy, drunkenness, and wild parties."

But as we saw in the Introduction, once we completely surrender our lives to Christ, the Holy Spirit resides within us to change us spiritually. From that day forward, all our desires become Christ-centered due to our "reformatted" governing disposition.

When pride separated us from God, we embraced the notion we had adequate righteousness in our merit. Many think about saying it, but only a few are brazen enough to say to the Lord: "Who are you to question my goodness? Don't you know who I am or what I've done?" The same attitude exists in those who retort when invited to church: "I don't go to your church because there are so many hypocrites there!"

In citing Proverbs 3:34, James rightly observes that God "resists the proud, but He gives grace to the humble" (James 4:6). Thus, we cannot produce freedom from sin when our heart is filled with pride and self-righteousness. That heart craves those things that offend God and harm people.

When we humbly submit our hearts and lives to the Lord, He frees us from sin. We are no longer slaves bound to living a life of sin and pleasing the self. Instead, we possess the unlimited freedom to live out a fulfilling, abundant life the Lord has prepared for us as King David illustrates in Psalm 23 (NLT):

> The LORD is my shepherd; I have all that I need. He lets me rest in green meadows; He leads me beside peaceful streams. He renews my strength. He guides me along right paths, bringing honor to His name. Even when I walk through the darkest valley, I will not be afraid, for you are

close beside me. Your rod and your staff protect and comfort me. You prepare a feast for me in the presence of my enemies. You honor me by anointing my head with oil. My cup overflows with blessings. Surely your goodness and unfailing love will pursue me all the days of my life, and I will live in the house of the LORD forever.

No longer in bondage, fear, guilt, and shame, we are free to choose the wholesome, Godly things that eluded us before. Now free to strive for spiritual maturity by saying no to sin, *Satan*, and self, we say yes to fasting, praying, reading God's Word, becoming active in a local church, fellowshipping with other Christians, and using our spiritual gifts to serve our church and community.

We have the freedom to go anyplace and do anything that honors the Lord and benefits others and ourselves. We are free to have fun, play, work, study, serve, give, laugh, cry, and be truly transparent and authentic in every way without being driven to fulfill our dysfunctional cravings that tend to hurt or endanger others and ourselves.

Although I have not arrived, there have been many wonderful changes in my spiritual journey where the Lord has set me free from pride, unforgiveness, selfishness, anger, guilt, fear, worry, lust, and other sins over the years.

But, I have truly been extremely blessed to have watched the Lord work in the hearts and lives of so many people to free them from drug addiction, sexual addiction, greed, guilt, shame, and other forms of compulsive addictive behavior. To have played a role in their process of spiritual development was truly an honor.

It was both amazing and gratifying to see and hear about former "addicts" being in the presence of their former "connections" completely "free" to show and tell of the transforming power of Jesus.

(A dear friend, who is now with the Lord, spent his remaining years being active in his church and also sharing his faith with relatives, friends, and acquaintances who were part of his sinful past with great effectiveness.)

Truly, we are free from worrying about what we did (or did not do) because the blood of Christ has covered it all. We are no longer bound by the guilt, shame, or emotional and psychological scars associated with our tragic past. The Lord reassures us we are forgiven, and He provides us with the comfort we need to overcome all things as He did (Psalm 30:5, John 16:33, Revelation 21:4).

Another benefit of forgiveness is our peace with God.

Peace with God

Through the vicarious and efficacious work of Jesus Christ, God deems us as having satisfied all of His righteous standards; suitable to have eternal, holy, and loving fellowship with Him according to Romans 5:1–2:

> Therefore, having been justified [*Justification*] by faith, we have peace with God through our Lord Jesus Christ, through whom also we have access by faith into this grace in which we stand, and rejoice in hope of the glory of God.

In addition, through Jesus' perfect work, we also have peace with God as observed here:

> [Peace with God] expresses the state of reconciliation (opposite to the state of condemnation, viii. 1), in the consequence of the removal of God's wrath and the satisfaction of His justice by the sacrifice of Christ, who is our Peace; Eph. ii. 14–16…Sin is the source of all discord and war between man and God, and between man and man; and hence there can be no peace until this curse is removed. All other peace is an idle dream and illusion. Being at peace with God, we are at peace with ourselves and with our fellow-men.[3]

Jesus says those who come to Him will not be cast out (John 6:37). Our peace with God is complete and eternal. We have been accepted into the presence of God and are no longer at odds with Him because of our sinful past.

Earlier we looked at Romans 6:23 and noted the wages of sin is death. Someone had to die, and Jesus did so. This is why the latter part of that verse states: "But the gift of God is eternal life in Jesus Christ our Lord."

Peace with God translates into a clear conscience that frees us from our past and opens new and exciting possibilities for our future.

With His peace, we now are free to express positive, constructive feelings toward God, others, and ourselves. Over time, our lives affirm there is no condemnation for those who are in Christ. We grow in His grace by walking, not according to the flesh but according to the Spirit as Romans 8:1–2 teaches.

When we have peace with God, we can be at peace with others and ourselves. Here, we do not seek to avenge, harbor grudges, or express ill will toward the people who may have wronged us in the past. Nor do we express ill will toward those who are of a different color or culture. Instead, we give them all a "clean slate" and treat them as though they are precious in God's sight—just as He does for us.

Sometimes *the Enemy* (or *Devil*) will use our negative experiences to perpetuate the lie we are worthless and cannot be loved and forgiven. People who struggle in this area will often say something like: "God will never love or forgive me...*You don't know what I've done!*"

We should always be mindful our past is immaterial since it has been erased and forgotten by the cross as Colossians 2:14 (NLT) states: "He canceled the record of the charges against us and took it away by nailing it to the cross."

The Lord knows us better than we know ourselves. He is aware of those "secret" sins no one else knows about. Yet He is willing to love, accept, treasure, value, and forgive us. Thus, we should be all the more willing to love, accept, treasure, value, and forgive ourselves.[4]

Our peace with God is the foundation on which our being, identity, choices, and destiny can be changed forever.

In this Chapter, we explored our forgiveness in Christ. In the next Chapter, we will look at how Christ provides us ultimate assurance.

Notes

[1]See: The Jewish Publication Society, *Tanakh: The Holy Scriptures: the New JPS Translation According to the Traditional Hebrew Text*, (Philadelphia: JPS, 1985) 88 notes a, b, c; 92 note a.

[2]Geisler, Normal L. *Christian Apologetics*, 5th ed., (Grand Rapids: Baker, 1991) 331.

[3]Lange, J.P. and F.R. Fay, "The Epistle of Paul to the Romans," in the *Commentary of the Holy Scriptures: Critical, Doctrinal and Homiletical*, trans., J.F. Hurst, P. Schaff and M.B. Riddle, 7th ed., vol. 10, (Grand Rapids: Zondervan, 1980) 160.

[4]Our active participation in a recognized Christian clinical treatment ministry or a certified recovery program in conjunction with a spiritual growth program within a local church can help us heal from the physical and emotional scars we sustained from an abusive past. It can also help us progressively escape the compulsive/addictive habits that keep us from reaching our full potential in Christ. Here, developing and maintaining a support and accountability network can help ensure we stay on a path that will lead us toward spiritual, emotional, and psychological healing and wholeness.

Chapter Two

Chapter 2
In Christ, We Have Ultimate Assurance

A Fleeting Illusion

The word "assurance," conjures ideas of personal and/or organizational safety and well-being. Here, our peace of mind increases or diminishes according to the confidence we have in the people and/or systems we use to provide security.

Research has shown a substantial increase within the corporate and personal security industry in recent years. For example, in 2018 alone the global security services industry should reach $220.9 billion US Dollars.[1]

This to accommodate our increasing need for personal and commercial surveillance systems, smoke and temperature detection, intrusion systems, fear of terrorism, personal security devices, cyber/data security, and theft control to protect the people and property we care about.

In addition, the US Department of Justice reports $28.8 billion in federal expenditures although the estimates for operating all federal, state, and local jails are approximately 80 billion dollars.[2]

Although I have spent much of my life behind "the razor wire" sharing the Lord with those who had been adjudicated there to "protect" the public from peril or loss, I have realized that all man-made security measures will never provide us with ultimate assurance.

Hackers, hijackers, electronic system failures, operator error, internal staff collusion, and "acts of God" can negate or bypass the security protocols causing a breach in the most advanced systems.

Since September 11, 2001, when the Twin Towers were attacked and destroyed, there has been heightened public interest to secure people, data, and property. However, each year there are telling instances of unauthorized exposure of personal information, loss of property, and the unfortunate loss of life as well. Life's capriciousness and uncertainty render earthly assurance a fleeting illusion.

Jesus warns about our feeble attempts to preserve earthly treasures in Matthew 6:19–21:

> Do not lay up for yourselves treasures on earth, where moth and rust destroy and where thieves break in and steal; but lay up for yourselves treasures in heaven, where neither moth nor rust destroys and where thieves do not break in and steal. For where your treasure is, there your heart will be also.

We can find ultimate assurance in Jesus Christ who gives lasting security along with faithful and enduring promises.

We Have Security

Two views on the eternal security of the believer have been debated for years. One group feels we who believe in Jesus Christ cannot be sure we will endure to the end. Some will renounce their faith in Christ entirely. This group feels that for many, obtaining eternal life will not happen.

However, I take the opposing view. We who are in Christ will endure to the end. According to this view, our eternal life is both certain and secure.

The fundamental difference between these two views is where we place our emphasis. Thus, where we put our faith and confidence determines our point of view.

The emphasis in the former view is on our capricious human will and our finite strength. Here, it is up to us to hold on to Christ the best way _we_ can as we face life's uncertainties in our strength.

In the second view, we focus on God's infinite power and providence. Here, it is up to God to hold on to us the best way _He_ can as we face life completely dependent on His strength.

Isaiah wrote about God's sustaining power: "But those who wait on the LORD shall renew *their* strength; They shall mount up with wings like eagles, They shall run and not be weary, They shall walk and not faint" (Isaiah 40:31).

Patient endurance is more about the Lord's omnipotence and faithfulness demonstrated toward His precious children than it is about our finite and uncertain attempts to hold on to Him.

Article Eleven entitled: "The Perseverance of the Saints," of the *New Hampshire Confession* describes God's power and providence:

> We believe the Scriptures teach that such as are truly regenerate, being born of the Spirit, will not utterly fall away and perish, but will endure to the end; that their persevering attachment to Christ is the grand mark which distinguishes them from superficial professors; that a special Providence watches over their welfare; and that they are kept by the power of God through faith unto salvation.[3]

We endure because our focus is on Christ, the Good Shepherd, whose providence watches over us while His power keeps us.

Here the difference between those who make a verbal profession of Christ as Savior and those who believe and receive Him as Lord is clearly seen. God assures those who confess Him with their mouths and believe in Him with their hearts as it states in Romans 10:9–10.

However, those people who merely profess with their mouths, and do not believe with their hearts are merely going through the motions. They have not experienced the spiritual transformation Christ provides, and they do not have fellowship with God.

When the Lord returns, He will banish them from His presence forever (Matthew 7:21–23). These will not endure because they are not of Christ, and He never knew them, as John explains:

> They went out from us, but they were not of us; for if they had been of us, they would have continued with us; but they went out that they might be made manifest, that none of them were of us (1 John 2:19).

We who _profess and believe_ are those who find hope, strength, and victory in Jesus Christ. We are certain to steadily progress along these mundane earthly shores until we reach our glorious heavenly home. Just as Proverbs 4:18 tells us, "But the path of the just is like the shining sun, That shines ever brighter unto the perfect day." *Amen!*

The day after He fed them, a crowd sought the Lord so that He could feed them again. Jesus explained He was the *Bread of Life* and those who would follow Him would never hunger or thirst (John 6:35).

Then to their astonishment, He went on to say He would raise us up "at the last day" (John 6:40). Here, Jesus was declaring He is capable of meeting all our spiritual and physical needs in this life and the next.

The crowd protested vehemently, insisting that what Jesus was proposing was too difficult for anyone to understand or accept. As the crowd left, they took many of His professed followers with them (see: John 6:60, 66).

Then the Lord turned to His disciples and asked if they were going to leave as well. Peter replied:

> Lord, to whom shall we go? You have the words of eternal life. Also we have come to believe and know that you are the Christ, the Son of the living God (John 6:68–69).

No one but Jesus Christ loves us so deeply, gives of Himself so freely, and keeps us so completely throughout this life and into the next.

Jesus Christ is not merely our security because in Him we have the embodiment of all of God's promises. In this way, we will pursue Him always because He delivered us from a life of sin and presents us before God as our everlasting all in all.

Faithful and Enduring Promises

As the Children of Israel were making their way through the forty years of *Wilderness Wanderings*, they traveled northward along the eastern side of the Dead Sea and the Jordan River where they encountered Balak who was the King of Moab.

The Moabites were descendants of Lot, the nephew of Abraham (Genesis 11:26–27; 19:37). Balak was afraid of an invasion from the Israelites and hires Balaam, son of Beor to place God's curse on the Israelites. Balaam was famous for blessing and cursing people, but God promised Abraham that He would bless his descendants (Israel) in Genesis 12:1–3.

Thus Balaam was moved by God, not to curse Israel, but to bless them repeatedly instead. To explain his actions to Balak, Balaam makes this statement in Numbers 23:19–20:

> God is not a man, that He should lie, nor a son of man, that He should repent. Has He said, and will He not do? Or has He spoken, and will He not make it good? Behold, I have received a command to bless; He has blessed, and I cannot reverse it.

It is comforting to know we serve a faithful, loving God who will not rescind His promises to provide all our needs according to His riches in glory — through Christ Jesus our Lord (Philippians 4:19).

After His baptism, our Lord went on a forty-day fast in the wilderness where *Satan* tempted Him. *Satan* challenged Him to turn the rocks into bread to satisfy His ravenous appetite and to renounce His call to receive all the glory of every kingdom on earth. *Satan* then overstates the role of angels protecting us as described in Psalm 91:11-12:

> "For He shall give His angels charge over you, to keep you in all your ways. In their hands they shall bear you up, lest you dash your foot against a stone."

The Psalmist never implied we have the license to jump off tall structures and rely on the angels to protect us. Nor did he imply we have carte blanche and get everything we want.

God will always have a far better perspective than the one we have, and He will do what is best in every situation. In Matthew 7:11, Jesus stated we know how to give good gifts to our children as parents, but God surpasses our ability.

Sometimes children do not get what they want because it is not good for them. Here, a child might ask to go somewhere or do something unsafe. A teenager might ask for a new car or permission to stay out late so that they can "hang out" with friends.

From the child's perspective, they may be convinced that what they want is in their best interest. However, the loving parent (or guardian) will have a far better understanding of what is best and will respond properly.

Similarly, God has a better view of what is best for us. His perspective is eternal and omniscient, and His thoughts are transcendent and flawless. With goodness and mercy, He responds in our best interest every time.

We will never get everything we want because that would not be in our best interest. Instead, God supplies our needs and gives us those things that allow us to accomplish His will.

We can ask confidently with a sincere, humble, reverent, selfless, and Christ-honoring posture. As we seek His *Kingdom* and righteousness first, we will experience His eternal peace, comfort, joy, and satisfaction (Matthew 6:33).

Our heavenly Father gives us good gifts in harmony with His will for us and a loving relationship with us as these writers observe:

> God is far more interested in a love relationship with you than He is in what you can do for Him. He will guide you to

do things. But even as you do those things, He will be the One at work through you to accomplish His purposes.[4]

Because the Lord has promised to keep us to the end, we can know the creator and sustainer of the heavens and the earth will keep His word.

God Sustains Us

While on earth, our Lord submitted Himself to God and resisted the Devil successfully. As we emulate the Lord, James 4:7 teaches we too can "resist the Devil, and he will flee from us."

Because Christ persevered and triumphed, we have the victory with the promise that no weapon formed against us will prosper (Isaiah 54:17). He dispatches His angels to keep us from danger, while His Holy Spirit dwells within to comfort us (John 14:16–18).

We are not invincible, for even the Lord's *Apostles* were persecuted and martyred. Nevertheless, eternal blessing is certain because we belong to the Lord, whether we are living in this world or have gone to the next. He sustains us through our persecution and suffering while protecting us from *Satan* and the other forces at work against us (Romans 14:8, Revelation 14:13).

The apostle John was the last remaining disciple. While in exile on the Isle of Patmos, he had time to reflect on the three years he shared with our Lord, the other disciples (now gone), as well as Pentecost and the growth of the New Testament church. Despite the persecution from the tyrannical Roman emperors, John did not renounce his faith. Instead, he persevered, just as the Lord predicted:

> Now I am no longer in the world, but these are in the world, and I come to You. Holy Father, keep through Your name those whom You have given Me, that they may be one as We are. While I was with them in the world, I kept them in Your name. Those whom You gave Me I have kept; and none of them is lost except the son of perdition, that the Scripture might be fulfilled (John 17:11-12).

There may be times when persecution and adversity cause us to doubt the Lord. As in the case of the three Hebrew boys presented in Daniel 3, we may find ourselves in a "fiery furnace."

But we can be assured God has not abandoned us. He will give us the extraordinary resolve to count it all joy because our unspeakable treasure is not on the earth—it is in Heaven.

Hardships do not negate God's love, grace, and mercy, nor do they reveal His desertion because nothing can separate us from His love. In the final analysis, all the things we experience will work together for our good (Romans 8:28).

Our toils and disappointments serve as constant reminders of the presence of sin in our world, which contrasts His magnificent *Kingdom*. There, all our toil and suffering will be forgotten instantly the moment we see Jesus Christ in His full majestic splendor (Revelation 21:3–4).

The Bible assures us we can be steadfast and ever vigilant in pursuing our incorruptible inheritance because we are kept by God's power "through faith unto salvation, ready to be revealed in the last time" (1 Peter 1:3-5).

This Chapter explored out assurance in Christ. The next Chapter will present our purpose and identity in Christ.

Notes

[1]For further discussion, see: Statista: The Statistics Portal, "Security Services Industry in the U.S. - Statistics & Facts." (accessed June 21, 2018); available from https://www.statista.com/topics/2188/security-services-industry-in-the-us, and Lucintel: Insights That Matter, "Growth Opportunities in the Global Security Services Industry." March 2013, (accessed June 21, 2018); available from http://www.lucintel.com/security-services-market-2018.aspx.

[2]Projected collateral costs for victims, families, children, and communities exceed $500 billion dollars. See: Huffington Post "Politics, The Full Cost of Incarceration In The U.S. Is Over $1 Trillion, Study Finds" 09/13/2016 05:01 pm ET, (accessed June 21, 2018) available from: https://www.huffingtonpost.com/entry/mass-incarceration-cost_us_57d82d99e4b09d7a687fde21, and Michael McLaughlin, et al., "The Economic Burden of Incarceration in the U.S." WP#AJI072016, (St. Louis: Institute for Advancing Justice Research and Innovation, Washington University, October 2016) available from https://advancingjustice.wustl.edu/SiteCollectionDocuments/The%20Economic%20Burden%20of%20Incarceration%20in%20the%20US.pdf, and the U.S. Department of Justice, "FY 2018 Budget Request at a Glance: Discretionary Budget Authority." (accessed June 21, 2018) available from https://www.justice.gov/jmd/page/file/968216/download

[3]See: Edward T. Hiscox, *The Standard Manual for Baptist Churches* (Philadelphia: American Baptist Publication Society, 1951) 67, and J. Newton Brown, *A Baptist Church Manual*, 37th ed., (Valley Forge: Judson, 1983) 15.

[4]Blackaby, Henry T. and Claude V. King, *Experiencing God* (Nashville: Broadman & Holman, 1994) 23.

Chapter Three

Chapter 3
In Christ, We Have Purpose and Identity

Fearfully and Wonderfully Created

In the beginning, as God was completing His *Creation* of the Heaven and the earth, He created man and woman and placed them in the *Garden of Eden*. But before performing His crowning achievement, God said:

> "Let Us make man in Our image, according to Our likeness; let them have dominion over the fish of the sea, over the birds of the air, and over the cattle, over all the earth and over every creeping thing that creeps on the earth" (Genesis 1:26).

Concerning our being made in the image of God, one commentator makes this observation:

> It is clear that man, as God made him, was distinctly different from the animals already created. He stood on a much higher plateau, for God created him to be immortal, and made him a special image of His own eternity. Man was a creature with whom his Maker could visit and have fellowship and communion. On the other hand, the Lord could expect man to answer Him and be responsible to Him. Man was constituted to have the privilege

of choice, even to the point of disobeying his Creator. He was to be God's responsible steward on earth, to work out his Creator's will and fulfill the divine purpose.[1]

The Psalmist describes us as being "fearfully and wonderfully made" in Psalm 139, and also notes:

> You made all the delicate, inner parts of my body and knit me together in my mother's womb...You saw me before I was born. Every day of my life was recorded in your book. Every moment was laid out before a single day had passed (Psalm 139:13–16 NLT).

Fearfully (Hebrew: *yare*) explores the idea of one standing in awe or rendering respect toward what God created.[2] In other words, fearfully is being in awe or recognizing a "mystery" that is special or unique, which we could *never* recreate as finite humans. Only an omniscient, omnipotent God can combine blood, bone, tissue, and flesh with His Spirit to create such special creatures as human beings.

Wonderfully (Hebrew: *pala*) conveys the idea of being separate or distinct.[3] Here, not only are the internal components of the human body separate but also distinct. (The Apostle Paul uses the human body metaphor to show how we

Christians are many members, yet we comprise one cohesive body in Romans 12:3–5.)

Yet in the grander scale, we humans are separate and distinct from — special from *all* other created beings just as God is special and unique; separated from all others. When He breathed in us "the breath of life," He purposely and deliberately imparted this distinction within us giving us an eternal human spirit (Genesis 2:7).

Genesis 2:15 states the Lord placed Adam in the Garden of Eden to manage and cultivate it. Ours is a solemn stewardship because we have dominion over the land, air, and aquatic creatures and the responsibility to cultivate vegetation, minerals, and water for its proper use and our benefit.

Colossians 1:16–17 tells how the Lord created all things, including us. But, I am saddened by those who do not see themselves as His greatest creation, for we are greater than Mount Everest, the Grand Canyon, Aurora Borealis, Victoria Falls, Table Mountain, the Barrier Reef, the Amazon Rainforest, the magnificent Redwoods, and the sun, moon, and stars combined — *in God's eyes*.

Through His Creation, we see God's majesty and design, in the most intricate detail to invoke our happiness and well-being. Genesis 1:31 tells us God considers *all* His creation to be "very good!"

The Psalmist also declares God designed us to be lower than the angels, and yet we are crowned with glory and honor with all things under our feet (Psalm 8:5). Truly, God has given us an amazing pedigree that is up to us to accept.

Nevertheless, we must never let our pride and sense of self-importance deceive us into thinking or feeling we are God ourselves. He is the Creator, and we are the created. Psalm 36:6 tells us God preserves (*Preservation*) the earth and all that is in it as this writer observes:

> Preservation is that continuous agency of God by which He maintains in existence the things He has created, together with the properties and powers with which He has endowed them...Preservation implies a natural concurrence of God in all operations of matter and of mind...Without His concurrence, no person or force can continue to exist or to act.[4]

The Lord wants us to be good stewards over His creation. However, when we spend our time in futile attempts to "save the planet," or "save the whales," or "save the rainforests," it amounts to fanaticism because "saving" what God created and preserves is beyond our human capacity. It is not our job to save the planet...*it's His alone*.

We are fallible and finite creatures who rely on God's preservation. For we cannot stop the earth from turning on its axis, nor can we stop the rain from falling; we cannot control the wind or stop the oceans from roaring. It is the Lord who does as all these things and more as Nehemiah 9:6 states (my emphasis):

> You alone are the LORD; You have made heaven, The heaven of heavens, with all their host, The earth and everything on it, The seas and all that is in them, *And You preserve them all.* The host of heaven worships You.

I believe our time would be better served if we focused on the things we can control instead of wasting time trying to meddle with things God controls more than adequately. We need to remember He's got it and us too.

God's marvelous creation also provides us with the undeniable evidence of His existence and loving care. The Psalmist observes the heavens declare His glory, and the skies above are the visual displays of His awesome craftsmanship (Psalm 19:1). Because of the undeniable witness of His creation, those who brazenly and defiantly scoff at His existence have no excuse on the day when they will account for "every idle word" (Matthew 12:36).

Parenthetically, made in His image also means we can choose where we will spend our eternity; whether in Heaven with the Lord or in Hell separated from Him. Jesus describes Hell as a place where there is weeping and gnashing of teeth; where the tormenting worms never die and the raging fire is never quenched (Matthew 13:42, Mark 9:48).

I believe the "weeping and gnashing of teeth" will be a self-imposed human torment to some degree. Because unfortunately, Hell is the place where atheism and agnosticism will no longer exist because everyone there will instantly become "believers" in God's existence and His redeeming love and grace freely extended to everyone through Jesus Christ. But they will spend eternity regretting not taking advantage of it – *when they were alive and had the opportunity.*

Unlike any other created being, we can choose to live a noble life that reflects our Creator's dignity to affect eternal changes in our lives and others around us. Thus, we should never consider ourselves to be mistakes or afterthoughts. We are special and unique persons who fulfill His perfect, eternal design for the universe. God created you, with all your complexity, to function according to His design: to bring Him honor, not the *Enemy*.

Our minds control our cognitive and anatomical functions. We should use them for proper thoughts, feelings, perceptions, and memories.

Isaiah 26:3–4 (NLT) is clear about what happens to those whose thoughts and minds are properly fixed on the Lord:

> You will keep in perfect peace all who trust in you, all whose thoughts are fixed on you! Trust in the LORD always, for the LORD GOD is the eternal Rock.

We also read in Philippians 4:8 (NLT):

> And now, dear brothers and sisters, one final thing. Fix your thoughts on what is true, and honorable, and right, and pure, and lovely, and admirable. Think about things that are excellent and worthy of praise.

We are to use our bodies as examples of God's love and goodness in the world and never as the *Enemy's* weapons for death and destruction. We are God's crowning achievements of creation and salvation. Thus, we are responsible for living out—to the best of our ability—the noble plan He has specifically designed for each of us before we were born.

Satan's job is to confuse and distort God's perfect plan by telling us our differences indicate we are flawed and worthless. He has convinced many of us that we are "ugly" and/or we "won't amount to anything." As result, many of us believe we will be "nothing but failures" in this life.

But these are lies for no two of us are exactly alike by design. God created us differently, much as if the pieces of a jigsaw puzzle that when assembled create a beautiful portrait of His love, redemption, and glory.

God's Purpose and Grace

Although we are created in the image of God to fulfill His divine purpose, many of us have assumed a false identity to achieve our God-given purpose. God designed us to express our emotions freely. Yet we put on facades in order not to show "weakness," to "be a real man," or "take it like a man."

To some, being strong means doing whatever it takes to get the newest, biggest, or best thing they can have. But, it's often at the expense of a poor, unsuspecting victim's physical, financial, or emotional well-being. Here, we equate being strong with obtaining "the good life" through self-centered extravagance, sexual prowess, drug and alcohol abuse, tyranny, and assault.

Whether the abused and exploited victims are traumatized physically and emotionally is irrelevant because "it's a dog-eat-dog world" where "only the strong survive." Thus, the "ends will always justify the means" because "it's not personal; it's only business."

I can remember when honesty and integrity stood for something in our society. Now, lying, cheating, and stealing have become accepted behavior, even for some professing Christians. I believe they are like a troubled sea, where there is neither rest nor peace (Isaiah 57:20–21).

Many people try to discredit our God-given purpose, but God has not. His is still creating offspring who will do justly, love mercy, and walk humbly before Him each day (Micah 6:8).

Second Timothy 1:9 tells us God has "saved us and called *us* with a holy calling, not according to our works, but according to His own purpose and grace which was given to us in Christ Jesus before time began."

Jesus declared He was the light of the world, and anyone who followed Him would "not walk in darkness but would have the light of life instead" (John 8:12). Thus, He affirmed His righteousness and ours as well.

As the Lord's branches, we can yield moral fruit consistently, just as He declared: "I am the vine, you *are* the branches. He who abides in Me, and I in him, bears much fruit; for without Me you can do nothing" (John 15:5).

God's purpose is that we contrast the prevalent, sinful lifestyles of those who celebrate pretense and reward dishonesty by sharing a compelling

Christian witness as being more than conquerors to those we encounter in our personal and social lives.

As I stated earlier, I spent much of my life serving in places where the message of Jesus Christ was shared with wonderful, transforming results. However, I must confess that during my tenure—particularly in the last ten years—I was grieved by the changing age demographics of our clientele.

There was an influx of a younger and more violent profile who I felt had their entire lives before them. To me, they should have been at their high school prom or graduation, getting ready for college, working, or raising a family—not spending the next fifty or sixty years of their lives in prison. (As my "public service" announcement: I am not knocking the prison system. It is used as a consequence for those who engage in lawbreaking and violent behavior. The Bible is full of accountability models for committing crime and restitution for those who are the victims. Whether we need improvements in our criminal justice system is another discussion.)

Yet, it seemed like more and more I was telling them I had no way of knowing what God had in store for them. Perhaps it was becoming a high school or college graduate, doctor, lawyer, musician, book author, minister, or a better son or daughter, spouse, or parent. Ultimately, it was not to be where they were emotionally, psychologically, or spiritually. God's plan for them was "exceeding and abundantly above" all that they could ever imagine (Ephesians 3:20).

Many of them listened as I related my story as an African-American from an impoverished background whom the Lord has blessed to live out my calling as a minister. I also shared the sentiments of King David in Psalm 37:25: "I have been young, and now am old; Yet I have not seen the righteous forsaken, Nor His descendants begging bread."

Nevertheless, sometimes I can't help but feel that too many of us have somehow lost our sight of God's purpose for our lives and our true identity to live out our full potential as His children. Once we capture and embrace His perspective, we see we are the unique and significant parts of His wonderful master plan.

Sometimes, our pride, fear, and unforgiveness can be our greatest adversaries. Pride makes us think we can advance through life without the assistance of others when we need it. We are "self-made" by raising ourselves "by our bootstraps." Even Jesus asked for help when He enlisted the services of twelve men to serve as His *Twelve Apostles* who helped Him change the world forever.

Fear of the unknown can paralyze us in such a way we miss opportunities to experience God's plan to the fullest. During those last ten years, part of my responsibility was to listen, share, and provide counseling. I was amazed by the number of people I encountered who never ventured beyond their street and neighborhood and missed the opportunity to learn about people and cultures other than their own.

Unforgiveness stifles our productivity as we waste time serving as a self-appointed vigilante; hoping others "get what they deserve." All of us are guilty of committing sinful acts against God and each other, either directly by commission or indirectly by omission. None of us are "perfect" enough to encumber another person (or group) with the debt of unforgiveness because all of us are offenders whether we share the same culture, color, or language.

I have also noticed our society has become far more intolerant and sensitive about the words or physical gestures others express. I grew up in a society that taught: "sticks and stones may break my bones, but words will never hurt me" even in school. We seemed much more tolerant and respected the opinions of others who exercised their right of free speech. We seemed to have had "tougher skins" back then than we do today.

I am not condoning obscenity, bullying, and impropriety here, and I realize this will always be part of our culture. Yet, all of us have the right to express our opinion—without resorting to violence—even when it's not politically correct. People who insist their opinions are the only ones that matter; that the opinions of others are invalid are mere "bullies" acting as self-appointed censors, and this is terribly wrong.

I too have faced my share of offensive words and gestures used to define me. But I thank God my parents raised me not to let people define me. I have learned I am a child of a loving God who values me differently. He left His glorious throne to assume my sin by dying on a cross nearly two thousand years ago, He is with me, and He still cares for me today. Ultimately, it is what the Lord says and thinks about me that matters most.

As Christians, the Lord specially designed us to help and support each other. Otherwise, our alternative is to engage in more hostility and senseless violence. The Lord provides us with the resources we need to be more than conquerors as we live out His purpose for our lives.

More Than Conquerors

We are more than conquers when we exhibit Jesus' life and character. In Romans 8:37–39, Paul makes this bold assertion (my emphasis):

> Yet in all these things *we are more than conquerors through Him who loved us*. For I am persuaded that neither death nor life, nor angels nor principalities nor powers,

nor things present nor things to come, nor height nor depth, nor any other created thing, shall be able to separate us from the love of God which is in Christ Jesus our Lord.

As we live out our true purpose as children of God, we covenant with the Lord daily to walk after His Spirit and not our sinful impulses. The Holy Spirit within us enables the "who we are when no one is watching" to interact with God, others, and ourselves safely and appropriately.

This means making the effort each day to please God through faith and spiritual due diligence by willingly and purposely performing tasks and forming habits that help us to grow closer to God.

In a church setting under the guidance of pastors, teachers, and leaders, we can learn what role we play in being more than conquerors by living out the Beatitudes in His Sermon on the Mount (Matthew 5:3–12).

With humility (*poor in spirit*), we receive the *Kingdom of Heaven* as our repentance (*they that mourn*) helps us receive God's eternal consolation and forgiveness.

Our strength under control (*meek*) helps us secure all this world has to offer as God satisfies our yearnings for Him (*hunger and thirst after righteousness*).

We can show pity (*merciful*) to others around us because we are the benefactors of God's pity. Our wholesome demeanor (*pure in heart*) and our harmony with others (*peacemakers*) reflect the internal spiritual transformation that allows God to identify us as His children who will see Him face to face one day.

Because of our allegiance to Christ, we will be misunderstood, criticized, and mistreated (*reviled and persecuted*) at times. Yet we can rejoice because of our association with the Lord will lead to eternal bliss.

As we grow spiritually, we produce more *Fruit of the Spirit* (Galatians 5:22-23) as they are Spirit-driven and emanate from God.

Love, the centerpiece, is our ability to share an unselfish benevolence toward others consistently. Instead of being cold, irritable, and self-willed, we can be affable, courteous, and gracious — even toward those who have wronged us.

Our *joy* emerges from the calm delight we experience through our fulfilling relationship with the Good Shepherd, in whom we lack nothing in this life or the next.

We can seek to create and preserve harmonious relationships with others because the *Prince of Peace*, who reconciled us to the Father, lives within us. We can experience *peace* while persevering to the end which is our *long-suffering*.

We can show our *gentleness* as we express civility toward others by not insisting on having our way and by seeking what is in the best interest of others.

Goodness is our intervention in the lives of others in ways beneficial to them, just as our Lord does for us. *Faith* goes beyond mere belief in Christ to include our extraordinary faithfulness in our spiritual, moral, and secular dealings with others as well.

Meekness reflects our humble submission to God's will in everything, just as Christ did for us. *Temperance* is our ability to practice personal self-control when our lusts of the flesh crave gratification.

Our greatest challenges are never physical. They are spiritual and require our whole *Armor of God*. Here, the Lord gives us the ability to be strong by standing firm in the power of His unfailing might as outlined in Ephesians 6:10–18.

To cover our torso, we securely fasten our belt (*Girdle of Truth*) around our waist. It helps to secure our body armor (*Breastplate of Righteousness*) in place. As the Lord's soldiers, we emulate His truth, integrity, and reliability as we intentionally perform noble acts that show how honest and reliable we can be (Romans 12:17).

Our foot attire (*Gospel of Peace*) provides a firm foundation for us. Each day we grow more familiar with the truths and promises of the Bible so that the Holy Spirit can "call it to mind" those things that will help us navigate life's uncertainties as David observes, "Your Word is a lamp to my feet and a light to my path." Our diligent study and preparation allow us to share biblical truths that benefit others and us (Psalm 119:105, 2 Timothy 2:15).

Our *Shield of Faith* quenches the fiery darts hurled at us as the "substance of things hoped for, [and] the evidence of things not seen" as Hebrews 11:1 attests. Over time, it repels the caustic words, emotions, and circumstances that can discourage and derail our progress and allows us to continue on the path of victory we have in Christ.

Our *Helmet of Salvation* protects the head, our most important body part. We have no spiritual effectiveness unless we are Born Again. We cannot tell people what we do not know and cannot lead them where we have not been. Jesus says we become the "blind leading the blind" to ultimate destruction (Matthew 15:14). The Seven Sons of Sceva learned this lesson when they tried to cast out an evil spirit. The spirit attacked them so violently they were left battered, bruised, and naked (Acts 19:16).

We have one offensive weapon, which is our *Sword of the Spirit (Word of God)*. God says His words will accomplish what He pleases and prospers where it is sent (Isaiah 55:11) Jesus used it against *Satan* when tempted by responding: "It is written" (Matthew 4:1–11). We do not find our victory in our opinions or the opinions of others. We find it in the precious and powerful Word of God.

We always pray (*Prayer*) and are not to lose heart as our Lord teaches in Luke 18:1. The Holy Spirit aids us to pray without ceasing as well (1 Thessalonians 5:17). Sometimes urgent moments in our lives can produce deep, spiritual yearnings our words fail to express adequately. The Holy Spirit intercedes for us to express our urgent needs, wants, and desires to the Lord on our behalf (Romans 8:26).

Jesus commands us to pray in His name so that under His authority, we can have a close communion with God that prompts Him to do miraculous things on our behalf and for those we pray for (John 14:13–14).

In this Chapter, we looked at our purpose and identity. The next Chapter will present our eternal fellowship.

Notes

[1] Yates, Kyle M. Sr., "Genesis," in *The Wycliffe Bible Commentary*, ed. Charles F. Pfeiffer, 8th ed., (Chicago: Moody Press, 1972) 4.

[2] For further discussion see: Merril F. Unger and Williams White, "Fear," *Nelson's Expository Dictionary of the Old Testament*, in W.E. Vine, et al., *Vine's Expository Dictionary of Biblical Words*, rev. ed. (Nashville: Thomas Nelson, 1985) 79, and Andrew Bowling, "Yare," in the *Theological Workbook of the Old Testament*, ed. R. Laird Harris, et al., 2nd ed., vol. 1, (Chicago: Moody Press, 1981) 399–401, and C.F. Keil and F. Delitzsch, "Psalms," in *Commentary on the Old Testament in Ten Volumes*, ed. James Martin, reprint, vol. 5, (Grand Rapids: WB Eerdmans, 1984) 348–349.

[3] See: William Wilson, "Wonder," in *Wilson's Old Testament Word Studies*, re-edition, (Peabody: Hendrickson, 1990) 487, and Victor P. Hamilton, "Pala," in *Theological Workbook of the Old Testament*, ed. R. Laird Harris, et al., 2nd ed., vol. 2, (Chicago: Moody Press, 1981) 724.

[4] Strong, 410–411.

Chapter Four

Chapter 4
In Christ, We Have Eternal Fellowship

One in Christ

When professing Christians replace Christ-centered ideals with worldly ones, we lose our exceptional Christian witness. One example is prejudice which gives us an excuse not to live in peace and harmony with others. This is a manifestation of the depraved heart; not the fruit of the transformed heart which God gives us the moment we come to Christ.

Prejudice is not a new problem within the New Testament church. In 1 Corinthians 1:10-13, Paul scolds the church at Corinth for the four factions that emerged within it because Christ is not divided.

Peter faced a similar problem when just a mere fifty days after the Lord's Resurrection; on the Day of Pentecost, the Holy Spirit filled the believers. Peter preached his first sermon before a vast crowd assembled at Jerusalem, and 3,000 people became believers.

As the New Testament church grew, certain Jewish extremists (Judaizers) wanted to preserve Jewish tradition within Christianity. Gentile (non-Jewish) believers could no longer have reconciliation by faith in Jesus Christ alone; they had to keep God's law and Jewish traditions as well. (After all, these were God's chosen who safeguarded *Jewish Law*, and Christianity was a mere reflection of Judaism since Jesus Christ was a Jew.) Circumcision and observing other laws and rituals soon became mandatory components of the Christian faith for many Christians.

Then at Joppa, God reminded Peter that He shows no partiality and expects us to follow suit. After the vision, Peter ministered to the non-Jew Cornelius and his family, and there was a Pentecostal experience among the Gentile believers.

I feel sad there are far too many professing Christians who resist fellowshipping with people who do not share the same race, culture, or class, although we share the same Lord and Savior, Jesus Christ. Many communities seem to have Christian churches on every street corner that share the same form of worship.

How can we testify to the world that we are one body in Christ and yet maintain world-centered ideals as though we are soldiers guarding a military base in enemy territory?

The Bible depicts Christians as a united group, serving the one true God, as Paul writes:

> Endeavoring to keep the unity of the Spirit in the bond of peace. There is one body and one Spirit, just as you were called in one hope of your calling; one Lord, one faith, one baptism; one God and Father of all, who is above all, and through all, and in you all (Ephesians 4:3-6).

I believe it is possible for us as Christians to think and act as one body in Christ by focusing on the things that unite us rather than wasting time on minute points that divide us. By our faith in Christ, we have an unbreakable union that allows us to fulfill His prayer for unity that transcends culture, race, gender, color, or class:

> I do not pray for these alone, but also for those who will believe in Me through their word; that they all may be one, as You, Father, are in Me, and I in You; that they also may be one in Us, that the world may believe that You sent Me. And the glory which You gave Me I have given them, that they may be one just as We are one: I in them, and You in Me; that they may be made perfect in one, and that the world may know that You have sent Me, and have loved them as You have loved Me (John 17:20-23).

We who are in Christ are one body united in love, with the Lord Jesus Christ as our focus. Regarding the unity we have in Christ, this author writes:

> Christ's omnipresence makes it possible for Him to be united to, and to be present in each believer, as perfectly and fully as if that believer were the only one to receive Christ's fullness...Each believer has the whole Christ with him as his source of strength, purity, life; so that each may say: Christ gives all His time and wisdom and care to me. Such a union as this lacks every element of instability. Once formed, the union is indissoluble. Many of the ties of earth are rudely broken—not so with our union with Christ—that endures forever. Since there is now an unchangeable and divine element in us, our salvation depends no longer upon our unstable wills, but upon Christ's purpose and power.[1]

We are called to show genuine affection toward each other because, in Christ, we are a family. We share our joys and offer encouragement, support, and aid to each other when distressed because the Holy Spirit compels us to do so. As a Christian family, we can change the world around us as we show the following characteristics.

Fellowship

We are a diverse people with Christ at the center. God loves, saves, and treats us as equals while His Word and Spirit enable us to practice a loving fellowship (Greek: *koinonia*).[2] This miracle of simultaneous unity and diversity under the banner of Christ validates our distinctive message of God's grace and love. Christians yearn for opportunities to fellowship because we enjoy our interconnection as a Christian family.

The world is a cold, cruel, and lonely place where smiles are rare, and people are so busy they do not have time to establish and maintain connections. Among Christians, we make even strangers feel welcome as we let them share our world. Inviting them to join us for Sunday dinner, celebrating birthdays and special occasions, and attending events of mutual interest are ways we show the world we are a family where no one is a stranger or outcast.

Benevolence

We Christians have a shared responsibility to honor and prefer one another through our benevolence as Paul taught in Romans 12:10. Food pantries, benevolent funds, and other forms of giving allow us to bring tangible and meaningful aid to our distressed brothers and sisters.

God has given the giver and the recipient a tremendous responsibility within the Christian family. The giver is responsible for assisting their brother or sister in need because God's Spirit removes our apathy, indifference, and stinginess and confirm we are the extensions of God's caring hands.

God has also given the recipient a great responsibility. Here, the requester must have a legitimate financial need with no intent to deceive the donor. It would be unconscionable for any person to claim to have an emergency when the intent is to support high-risk behavior instead. The recipient must not exploit the giver by taking advantage of their generosity. Our God is a vengeful God, and He will severely punish anyone who exploits His precious children.

Here, financially supporting one's substance abuse, gambling habit, or some other non-emergency is bad. But it can never be a win/win proposition to pay for food, rent/mortgage, car note, utilities or other personal expenses, when the person asking feels entitled to have a "free ride" through life, or is too proud or lazy to perform an honest day's work.[3]

Encouragement and Affection

As we provide emotional and spiritual support to our brothers and sisters during crises, we show the entire world that ours is a caring community of faith through prayer and tangible and meaningful support. Here we become a listening ear, offer a shoulder to cry on, give a pat on the back, and provide wise counsel as needed.

We never "stockpile ammunition" for gossip against our brothers and sisters. Either we keep confidences safe, or we ask for permission to share with professionals better suited to address the issue so that it can be resolved appropriately.[4]

Jesus Christ is a friend who sticks closer than a brother, and He has equipped us to care for other Christians. We may disagree about dogma or our form of worship, yet, we look beyond our human-made differences to unite in Christ.

Expressing our affection is easy because we see each other not through our eyes, but through the eyes of Christ who was willing to lay down His life for His friends. We see this whenever we meet other Christians who may not share our race, culture, or language, yet we are attracted to them almost instantly and feel comfortable around them even though we have never met them before.

We share the same Lord, Jesus Christ, and His Spirit within us makes us one, just as He is one with His Father. In this way, we contrast the snobbery and prejudice the world accepts and embraces as we demonstrate a fellowship that dispels disharmony, hatred, and ill will by showing it is possible for a group of diverse people to coexist peacefully despite our differences. This is our distinct Christian witness that verifies our genuine fellowship with God.

Evangelism is never frustrated, nor is Christ's witness invalidated due to petty human divisiveness, as we proclaim God loves and seeks reconciliation with a sin-cursed humanity. We celebrate our diversity by treating each other with the utmost respect, acceptance, and honor. Our affection is not optional—it is compulsory.

The world craves this unifying message of acceptance of others through Christ, which offers us a glimpse of what Heaven will be like with its rich diversity of people united under the lordship of Jesus Christ. John saw our future while he was on the Isle of Patmos:

> After these things I looked, and behold, a great multitude which no one could number, of all nations, tribes, peoples, and tongues, standing before the throne and before the Lamb, clothed with white robes, with palm branches in their hands, and crying out with a loud voice, saying, "Salvation belongs to our God who sits on the throne, and to the Lamb" (Revelation 7:9-10).

Just as the Lamb's eternal glory unites us in Heaven and on earth, Jesus is returning for us at any moment. Because we are all precious in His sight, we can value each other equally and see each other through His gracious and forgiving eyes. In this way, we can show we are one in

Christ, and we all are blood-washed and blood-bought saints.

Communion with God

This earth is not our final destination. The Bible tells us we are mere pilgrims and strangers traveling through it. For some, the journey may be thirty years or less while others exceed the seventy-year benchmark given in Psalm 90:10. Whatever time we have, Job 14:5 tells us the Lord has determined the exact day and time of our death.

But while we await our departure, the Lord has promised everlasting communion with both He, and the Father through the Spirit. Before going to the cross, He comforts us with His promise to return:

> Don't let your hearts be troubled. Trust in God, and trust also in me. There is more than enough room in my Father's home. If this were not so, would I have told you that I am going to prepare a place for you? When everything is ready, I will come and get you, so that you will always be with me where I am (John 14:1–3 NLT).

Then just before the *Ascension*, He reassures us He would be with us forever...*most assuredly* (Matthew 28:20). His is an intimate, communion that lasts forever. For in Christ, we have the

Comforter who gently comforts, helps, guides, teaches, and secures us until we inhabit our eternal home (John 16:7–15).

The Lord is with you before you were born; shaping you in your mother's womb; planning your bright hope and expected end that will inspire others and bring honor to the Lord Jesus Christ (Jeremiah 29:11).

He is there as you open your eyes for the first time looking into the face of loving parents who carry you home from the hospital to love, nurture, care, and provide the things you cannot provide for yourself. Your earliest recollection is how they pray over you and tell you about God's eternal, loving, redeeming, and transforming love.

As a toddler, He is there when your parents provide medical treatment after you step on a rusty nail, and when someone needs to rescue your arm from the washing machine wringer. He is with you as you go to public school and make friends you are still connected with today. He is there as you explore the world around you; learning about people, places, and cultures different from your own, as your family moves across the country.

He is there when you are living in housing projects, and you learn how not to waste food; you learn how to warm your donuts in the oven to kill the ants before you can eat them. He is with you as you move several more times before He gives you a home where you find your "hideaway" and have regular personal devotions with God. There, you grow to experience His presence around you: sheltering, loving, caring, joyful, tender, and merciful as you also grow to experience the joys and sorrows associated with this life as well.

He accepts your invitation to come into your heart (Revelation 3:20), and He becomes your personal Savior and Lord. He is there as you declare your faith before the entire church family and are baptized a few weeks later. The water's chilly temperature does not dampen the warm radiance you feel in your heart knowing the Lord is pleased with you and your actions.

He is with you at church, filling the rafters with His glory while the choir sings songs of Zion:

> Blessed assurance, Jesus is mine! Oh, what a foretaste of glory divine! Heir of salvation, purchase of God, Born of His Spirit, washed in His blood.
>
> Refrain:
> This is my story, this is my song, Praising my Savior all the day long; This is my story, this is my song, Praising my Savior all the day long.[5]

In your adolescent years, He is with you while riding public transportation; sometimes seated in the vacant seat next to you, as you incessantly and voraciously read the small, blue, pocket Bible you kept in your shirt breast pocket

He helps you to grow spiritually at church as you help others there grow in their faith and understanding of Him. You help teach the Bible lessons, assist in training sessions, and lead Bible drills to help people become familiar with the contents of the Bible. You also serve in the choir and as a Junior Deacon in the weekly worship services.

He is there as you share your faith in the community. He leads you to go door-to-door, to visit the rescue mission, and to visit the prison because you want to tell men, women, boys, and girls about the God whom you have come to know and love deeply. You also work with underprivileged youth, hoping some of them looking for a role model will find it in the loving God you know as your heavenly Father.

He is there when a classmate invites you to accompany him to his house after school. You both walk to his home, an old Victorian in the city. Hours pass as you share and listen. But you can't help but notice the small hole in the front window in the living room, and although you never mention it, you wonder if it had been made by a bullet—directed at your host—recently.

He is there to help you properly discern the myriad of "voices" that beckoned you and your contemporaries during the turbulent era of the '60's within our country with: Vietnam, Civil Rights, Black Panthers, Nation of Islam, Berkeley, Woodstock, Hippies, Haight-Ashbury, "We Shall Overcome," "Say It Loud: I'm Black and I'm Proud," "Burn Baby, Burn," "Turn On," "Drop Out," "Sit-In," "Love In," "God Is Dead," JFK and Bobby, Martin and Malcolm, James Brown, Motown, The Beatles, Janis Joplin, and Jimi Hendrix; so many voices demanded your undivided attention.

Amidst all the turmoil, it was the Lord's gentle whisper that captivates you. With it, He leads you to trust in Him with all your heart, and not to rely on your finite understanding; to acknowledge Him in all your ways, so that He directs your paths, as Proverbs 3:5–6 teaches.

He is with you as you can't help but notice the vast difference between His love and the love you hear propagated by society. You see their form of love is selfish and sexually oriented as the slogan: "make love not war" that many of your friends espouse suggests. But God's love provides eternal purpose, meaning, and significance. It also gives fulfillment, direction, joy, peace, and true and lasting happiness as well. You learn that God's love means something, and it costs something: *His life and your submission.*

The Lord is there as you leave home as a young adult in search of ways to serve Him better. He is there to dry your tears on your first night away from home, and He is there to encourage you to pursue His plan for you. Soon He sends new friends and reassures you to "be strong and of good courage;" not afraid or dismayed; "for He is with you, wherever you go" (Joshua 1:9).

He is there as you make a new home for yourself. You see His reflection in the faces of your new family; your beloved wife and children with whom you share being born, first steps, going to school, after-school activities, learning to ride a bicycle, going to amusement parks, learning to drive a car, and sharing other activities together.

He strengthens you as your children fall in love…and out of love; go to dances, special events, mission trips, and sleep-overs; graduate high school; serve their country by joining the military; get married, and bring life into the world themselves as well. But before departing, and leaving you and your wife as "empty-nesters," you recall the times you prayed with them, shared your faith with them, and listened as they shared how the Lord was working in their lives also.

You see the Lord move on the hearts of your children as they publically declare their faith. You and your wife, who shares your faith in and love for the Lord, are happy knowing their personal experiences with the Lord will lead them on a marvelous journey that transcends this life and flows into the next.

The Lord is also with you as you visit the Lincoln Memorial, Ford's Theatre, the Reflecting Pool, the Smithsonian, and the Washington Monument in our Nation's Capital. He is with you as you and your wife stand on the Observation Deck atop the Empire State Building, and when you visit the Statue of Liberty, Times Square, and Central Park in New York together. He is with you both as you stand in awe of the roaring and majestic Niagara Falls, visit the USS Arizona Memorial in Pearl Harbor; later enjoying a Hawaiian Luau and some tropical fruit. As you travel, you are grateful to the Lord for His provisions and presence which allow you to enjoy fully the many wonders of His creation.

He protects you from danger; seen and unseen. Just as when the brakes fail on your ten-speed bicycle while you are coasting down a steep hill many years before, He protects you while you are driving on the interstate late one night when you suddenly awake from dozing off momentarily. The vehicle is still moving at the posted speed limit, and it is in the proper lane. Shocked and embarrassed by what just happened, you look over at your wife who's sleeping in the passenger seat, and you immediately sense the Lord has protected you, and you realize "all is well."

The Lord is there when your employer informs you that your services are no longer needed, and He is beside you when you receive hundreds of rejection letters and emails as you apply for work elsewhere. He is there to provide comfort and affirmation that you are still valuable and productive: "Even in old age they will still produce fruit; they will remain vital and green" (Psalm 92:14 NLT). Armed with His courage and strength, you pledge to continue serving the Lord to the very best of your ability for as long as you live.

The Lord is there as you become the first in your family to complete your college degree and later attend seminary. After twelve years of classroom study, you arrive at your third graduation ceremony. He is there as you pause to embrace your loving, supportive wife on the auditorium stage when you receive your hood and diploma. Then the seminary president presents you to the assembly as the *Rev., Dr. Floyd W. Bland, Sr.,* and you can't help but be humbled by what is happening. You are extremely grateful to the Lord for having done so many wonderful things for this: "poor black kid from the projects."

The Lord is there to comfort you when Dad, who raised you, and was truly your hero, goes home to be with the Lord. You miss your Dad, so the Lord reassures you that you will see him again in Heaven. But in the meantime, the Lord becomes your new "Dad."

In addition, He is there when your life comes full-circle as you move across the country to provide quality care, comfort, and safety for your Mom and Mama Clee (grandmother) during their remaining years. You have been raised to honor your parents, but these two are more than just your mother and grandmother. They are your best friends and role models whom you love, respect, admire...and dearly miss even today.

He is there as your aches, pains, shortened steps, and gray hairs accumulate. You realize soon you will see Him face-to-face and reunite with departed friends and loved ones. Then, you will experience His communion in its totality.

The Lord is with you, and each day you understand even more how your experiences with Him on earth are merely a foretaste of the eternal life that awaits you in His glorious *Kingdom*. The Lord is with you, and your faith begins and ends with Him. He is your hope, peace, expectation, your sun and shield, and your exceeding great reward (Genesis 15:1). He gives you "grace and glory, and no good thing will He withhold from you as you walk uprightly" (Psalm 84:11).

Our Lord provides the foundation on which our being, position, choices, and destiny are secured forever. For this reason, 2 Corinthians 5:7 states "we walk [with the Lord daily] by faith, and not by sight." With a humble, reverent, and sincere faith in Jesus Christ, we are certain to reach our glorious final destination.

He will be with us as we experience the pinnacle of His redemptive work of *Glorification*, where "the wicked cease from troubling, and the weary will be at rest" (Job 3:17). He will supply us with an immortal body that will allow us to experience His holy, eternal presence fully. Free from sin, pain, and disease, we will be completely capable of having eternal communion with God as we see Him "as He is" and are like Him (1 John 3:2).

We explored our eternal fellowship in this Chapter. In the next Chapter, we will explore how we are new creations in Jesus Christ.

Notes

[1] Strong, 801.

[2] See: W.E. Vine, "Fellowship," *An Expository Dictionary of New Testament Words*, in W.E Vine, et al., *Vine's Expository Dictionary of Biblical Words*, rev. ed. (Nashville: Thomas Nelson, 1985) 232, and Strong, James, "κοινωνια," *A Concise Dictionary of the Words in the Greek New Testament*, in *The Exhaustive Concordance of the Bible*, (Iowa Falls: Riverside, 1980?) 42.

[3] Here, giving would demonstrate poor stewardship. Instead, it would be best to help the person find an appropriate church ministry, Christian nonprofit organization, counseling service, or social service agency that would be better suited to address his or her needs.

[4] We are "duty bound" to report criminal behavior and/or possible threats that can endanger public safety.

[5] Osbeck, Kenneth. "Francis J. Crosby, Blessed Assurance," *101 Hymn Stories*, (Grand Rapids: Kregel, 1982) 42.

Chapter Five

Chapter 5
In Christ, We are New Creations

A New Perspective

When asked which was the greatest of all God's  Commandments, Jesus said there were two: we must love God with all our heart, soul, and mind, and love our neighbors to the same extent we love ourselves (Matthew 22:36-40, Mark 12:28-34, Luke 10:25-37).

The Lord's answer reveals His desire that we live in harmony with God, neighbors, and ourselves even when meeting our physical, social, and aesthetic needs. Altruism sustains and improves our quality of life while exploiting people and things for our sensual gratification does not.

One biblical example was Simon Magus who offered Peter money for the Holy Spirit's power. His intended to enhance his power and magic when the Holy Spirit was free to all who sought a real spiritual transformation (see: Acts 8:13-19). The term "Simony" or the buying and selling of the sacred and spiritual for material gain has been attributed to him.[1]

False teachers embrace a lawless form of Christianity through antinomianism (Greek: *anti*, meaning "against" *nomos*, meaning "law").[2] In antinomianism, no longer do the Word of God and the Holy Spirit direct a Christian's thoughts, words, and actions exclusively. Instead, whatever feels good (or whatever feels right) is considered with equal or greater value.

These fence sitters live conflicted lives trying to accommodate two diametrically opposed realities. One reality features Christ as Savior where His abundant and eternal life prevails. The other reality features *Satan*, the world, and self where a life of sin and debauchery prevails.

The Bible depicts the time just before our Lord's return as a lust-driven world of addictions, where iniquity abounds, and people no longer have a regard for their fellow human beings (see: Matthew 24:7, 2 Timothy 3:1–5).

Instead, using people and cherishing things will be the commonplace occurrence as people pursue the pride of life, the lust of the eyes, and the lust of the flesh with all fervor.

The pride of life is a self-centered obsession with power or influence without regard for the safety, and well-being of others. This is in stark contrast to God's design for power and influence, which is to maintain order, render justice, and help others in need.

When we succumb to sin, we turn our focus away from others and onto ourselves. With a new credo, "God helps those who help themselves," we often resort to satisfying our cravings at another person's expense.

The abuse of power over others manifests itself in physical and/or emotional abuse or assault. The pride of life can be as subtle as prejudice or as overt as war, and it can affect us directly or indirectly.

The lust of the eyes is coveting things of value for our aesthetic gratification. The love of money is one example of this. God wants us to use our money as a form of worship through tithes and offerings which express our appreciation to God for His providence while providing for His servants who minister to us.

God also wants us to use our money to show benevolence toward others who are less fortunate through charitable giving and to create wealth for ourselves as well. The lust of the eyes changes the purpose for money into selfish extravagance. We splurge on ourselves and are cold toward others in need of our generosity and compassion.

The lust of the flesh is the overindulgence of our sensual desires. Gluttony, substance abuse, and sexual immorality are all forms of this obsession. The Bible teaches sexual promiscuity devastates God's plan to sustain healthy, interpersonal relationships. Pre-marital sex, adultery, homosexuality, masturbation, pedophilia, rape, spying on partially clothed or naked people (voyeurism), and pornography are forms of what this writer calls *Sexual Idolatry:*

> For many, the powerful human drive for sex becomes the overriding passion of life. Kept in its proper place, sex is a marvelous means for a married couple to physically express their love to each other. However, when a person begins to indulge in some form of illicit sexual behavior, this passion can quickly get out of control...Thus, his sexuality and capacity to worship become fused into a corrupted, nearly irresistible drive to worship *at the altar of sexual idolatry.*[3]

Immorality has never been the identification badge that we as Christians can display brazenly and callously before the world. Our Lord Jesus Christ calls us to represent Him with moral and spiritual purity.

Through Christ, we now share a willingness to honor Him, serve others, and meet our needs safely and appropriately. When He transformed us from the inside out, He released us from the bondage of sin and gave us the ability to resist temptation as we walk in His Spirit.

There will be times when we yield to temptation. Yet our Lord supplies us with the power we need to resist making excuses to mask our sin.

In this way, He turns us from our destructive patterns of non-biblical or compulsive, addictive behavior as we rely on His Spirit to strengthen our faith walk each day.

A New Lifestyle

Over time, we can grow into morally astute practitioners of the Christian faith who refrain from exploiting others. With our growing moral consciousness, we produce the living fruit that validates our Christian witness, as this author writes:

> There must be a sincere change in one's lifestyle. A person who has genuinely repented will stop doing evil and begin to live righteously. Along with a change of mind and attitude, true repentance will begin to produce a change in conduct.[4]

Our God is morally and spiritually perfect, and glorious in His holiness. This trait encapsulates the very core of His being. The Old Testament word that describes something sacred or holy (Hebrew: *qados*) depicts God as the One who has a pure, undefiled quality of essence, which separates Him (or "cut off") from anything in His group or class.[5] He is the one, true, holy God!

The New Testament counterpart (Greek: *hagios*) describes God as pure, blameless, sacred; distinct from what is common or normal and conveys the idea of bestowing reverence.[6] Whether we study the Old or New Testament, the message is clear: holiness is predicated on God, who alone is pure, majestic, and glorious. In other words, our God is holy and without equal.

At Sinai, Moses asked God to show Himself. God warned him that one brief glimpse of His glory would be too much for any mortal. Instead, God placed Moses in a cleft on the mount. Then as He passed by, Moses bowed and worshipped and caught a brief glimpse of God's glory from behind. This brief glimpse illuminated Moses' face to the extent he veiled his face to keep from frightening others (Exodus 34:28-35, 2 Corinthians 3:12-18).

On the Mount of Transfiguration, Peter, James, and John were talking to Jesus when His clothing turned bright white. When a cloud overshadowed them, a voice thundered: "This is my beloved Son: hear Him!" (Mark 9:7).

After Pentecost, Peter and John healed the lame man at the Jerusalem Temple, and Acts 4:13 states:

> "Now when they saw the boldness of Peter and John, and perceived that they were uneducated and untrained men, they marveled. And they realized that they had been with Jesus."

These are not isolated incidents. When we express a sacred devotion or sanctity toward God (or *get real with God*), His captivating radiance becomes visible through us. Paul illustrates this kind of sacrificial living in Galatians 2:20:

> I have been crucified with Christ; it is no longer I who live, but Christ lives in me; and the life which I now live in the flesh I live by faith in the Son of God, who loved me and gave Himself for me.

He also makes a similar declaration in Colossians 3:1–4:

> If then you were raised with Christ, seek those things which are above, where Christ is, sitting at the right hand of God. Set your mind on things above, not on things on the earth. For you died, and your life is hidden with Christ in God. When Christ who is our life appears, then you also will appear with Him in glory.

In the Old Testament, God commands His people to be holy, just as He is holy (Leviticus 20:26). Likewise, in the New Testament, Jesus states we are to live our lives with "no part dark" (Luke 11:36).

One can only imagine the impact we'd make within our families, churches, communities, nation, and the world if more of us lived our lives with <u>no</u> part dark. It would certainly free us from all forms of bondage and exploitation. How much safer would our world be if we lived like this? *Simply incredible!*

As finite and fallible creatures, achieving His holiness (*Sanctification*) is impossible without His intervention. God's life-changing Spirit compels us to revere His creation with a sober view of His eternal being. This will help us pursue His moral and spiritual perfection with all sincerity and dedication.

With this new appreciation for God, we can no longer express indifference and ambivalence about our church involvement because we are driven to present a sincere, reverent, intentional Christ-centered way of living that involves our deliberate participation.

Our new life reflects the Spirit's work within us and our desire to grow closer to God in all phases of our lives. Much like a compass needle that points north because of the magnetic forces, our freedom in Christ points others to the Christ who lives in and works through us.

We also develop a strong sense of piety and reverence toward God while craving a deeper intimacy level in our fellowship with Him. Each day, it becomes easier to invite Him to reign in every area of our lives so that we can reflect His holiness.

God is a life-changing Spirit whose incredible majesty and splendor compel us to revere Him with a sober view of His eternal being. This helps us pursue His moral and spiritual perfection with all sincerity and dedication.

With this Spirit-driven, distinguishable lifestyle, we now can keep our word, speak the truth in love, and ask for help when we need it. Confiding in a pastor, a trusted, mature Christian friend, or a qualified professional can be invaluable to us as we seek to attain spiritual and moral balance.[7]

We obtain spiritual, emotional, and psychological harmony by growing "in wisdom, stature, and favor with God" and others as the Lord did (Luke 2:52). Now when we are tempted and fall into sin, we do not blame others or use flimsy excuses to escape accountability. Instead, we ask God for forgiveness, we reconcile with the offended person or persons, and we practice an improved moral and spiritual lifestyle.

Moreover, we exhibit emotional security and are not afraid, threatened, or intimidated by the status, abilities, accomplishments, or possessions of others. Envy has no place in our hearts when we interact with other people. Because we understand the Lord causes people to rise or fall, we should not waver from trusting His infinite wisdom and providence.

Psalm 37:23 states our steps are ordered by the LORD, who delights in our way. Since it is the Lord who directs and delights in our every step, we can never be proud, boastful, or haughty over our position or abilities because we are merely God's stewards. He blessed us with resources so that we can be a blessing to others, and He has every right to expect us to be faithful in our stewardship.

Ultimately, we understand God created us to perform a special work. Much like keys in the hands of a locksmith, we are designed to fit a particular "lock" that opens new doors for others and ourselves. Thus, each day presents new opportunities for the Lord to "reset" our lives and circumstances to accommodate His perfect will for us:

> The faithful love of the Lord never ends! His mercies never cease. Great is His faithfulness; His mercies begin afresh each morning. I say to myself, "The Lord is my inheritance; therefore, I will hope in Him! (Lamentations 3:22–24 NLT)

We realize the importance to protect, preserve, and strengthen our bodies through adequate rest, exercise, and diet. We reduce unhealthy levels of stress, abstain from drug and alcohol abuse, and engage in physical activities that honor Christ. We also provide a positive witness to others as good winners or losers because He is at the center of everything we do where ever we are making a difference within our global community.

Making a Difference

Home

In the home, we attend church, read God's Word, serve, pray, and play together as uniquely gifted members of one homogeneous entity where we handle each member with care. Here, everyone is safe from sexual, physical, and emotional abuse. We treat each other with dignity and respect and not as objects of personal gratification. We replace cutting, insensitive, and insulting remarks with comforting words and positive affirmations that serve to encourage and support each member.

Serving as the family's spiritual leader, husbands use Christ's love as the example to love their wives even to the extent of sacrificing their lives for them. Husbands and fathers lead in providing for the spiritual welfare of their families and by sharing their faith in the Lord with each member.

The more they give their love, time, and attention, the more they realize how important it is not to chase careers, wealth, possessions, electronic or mechanical "toys," and self-centered interests. Ultimately, they understand those material things that do not last are a poor substitute for a caring and listening husband and father. Wives can be submissive to husbands as they both share in the responsibilities of maintaining a Christ-centered home.

Parents and children practice well-defined roles: parents act like parents, and children act like children—*not vice versa!* Parents provide care and nurturing while raising their children properly. They refrain from hostility and condemnation by giving love, support, and affirmation while modeling a lifestyle that is true, reliable, and sincere before their children.

Parents also administer consistent and appropriate corrective discipline. Parents do not provoke their children to wrath but help them see there are grave consequences associated with wrong actions. In this way, they help their children learn how to function safely, respectfully, peacefully, and effectively in our global society.

Through their instruction and lifestyle, parents can train children in the way they should go so that they can remember their creator in the days of their youth (Proverbs 22:6, Ecclesiastes 12:1).

This will help children to pursue constructive, godly things instead of destructive, worldly things. With a developed understanding and appreciation for the things of God, children can be free to devote a lifetime of service to the Lord in whatever religious or secular vocation they pursue.

There may be times when children experience a "role reversal" as they provide "parental care and concern" for their parents who can no longer care for themselves adequately. In this way, children not only express a tangible and meaningful love and respect for their parents, but they also fulfill God's command to honor our fathers and mothers (Exodus 2:12).

The family is not exempt from sickness, poverty, death, and other life issues that affect us all. Even so, we can remain true to God and each other by trusting in the Lord Jesus Christ to meet every need.

Yet as the most intimate way to experience God and grow toward Christian maturity, God still uses the home to make a positive impact on the world through our shared love, sense of belonging, fun, service, commitment, and cooperation.

Church

The church is a reflection of God's eternal *Kingdom* where His righteousness prevails. Here, we worship, hear and/or learn God's Word, fellowship, serve, and observe our Lord's ordinances.

Church leaders provide pastoral care, biblical instruction, and help us identify and use our spiritual gifts and material resources to bring honor to the Lord Jesus Christ as well.

We submit to each other under the leadership of our pastors and elders because the Lord inhabits His holy temple where His people worship, honor, and serve Him faithfully.

Whether parishioners or guests, we can interact in ways that help others feel valued regardless of race, culture, wealth, age, gender, or social status. Social cliques and sexual, emotional, financial, or physical exploitation are not permitted because we assemble to celebrate our diversity and unity as fellow believers in Christ and show His church remains impervious to the gates of Hell.

Working

In the workplace, we represent the company and ourselves as God's faithful stewards. Thus, we are reliable and responsible with company resources, we submit to authority, we follow instructions, and we do not express petty sentiments toward our coworkers.

We are exemplary team players who celebrate the achievements and comfort the distresses of our colleagues. Never gloating or cynical, we maintain a positive demeanor even when we do not receive recognition for our work.

We are prompt, work hard, take only allotted breaks, leave when scheduled, and never defraud the company with bogus sicknesses or injuries to get time off or to collect disability payments.

Also, we refrain from using office equipment for personal use, and we submit honest, accurate reports and assignments. We never use our work time to catch up on our Bible study or witnessing.[8] As faithful and trustworthy stewards of the Lord's resources, we will receive His eternal commendation.

Learning

Yearning to better ourselves through formal interactive learning, we are respectful to our classmates, teachers, and administrators. We are punctual, study diligently, and practice being sociable and humble toward our classmates.

We do not cheat on exams or plagiarize another's work. We follow class instructions and directives, and we do not steal or misuse assigned school or library equipment and supplies. We also refrain from participating in activities that promote binge drinking, hazing, exhibitionism, and sexual promiscuity.

We are ever learning and complete our class assignments to prepare for our commencement into the world where our learning will enrich the lives of others.

In Our Communities

Once aliens, God reconciled us to Him when He called us out of darkness into His marvelous light (1 Peter 2:9). Using His example as our model, we can form and nurture meaningful relationships that can improve our social condition by advancing the causes of others and treating people with the respect and dignity they deserve.

We acknowledge we are created in God's image as equals and show it is possible to interact peacefully with others without bigotry and prejudicial lawlessness. We also treat others with sincerity, honor, and respect regardless of class or gender.

I am saddened by what seems to be heightening racial hostility in the US where people should express civility and understanding. I am a natural-born US citizen, and when I consider my history and that of my fore parents, there are those unfortunate issues and associated events, (i.e., slavery, prejudice, segregation, discrimination, etc.) that yet evoke rage from many of my people even today.

Although some feelings of rage may be justified, over the years, I have realized ours is _not_ a perfect world. Exploitation and victimization happen everywhere around the globe leaving me with the understanding there is much work to be done everywhere—even within my race.

I must be willing to accept that one particular race did not "corner the market" on victimization or being victimized. There were other races: Native American, Asian, Pacific Islander, Irish, Italian, Hispanic, etc., that have either imposed or faced discrimination, injustice, and hostility in this country as well.

Yet, I am grateful to the Lord to live in this country, which He has greatly blessed with many opportunities we often take for granted: to freely worship, to express opinions without censorship, to elect our representation, and to travel where we want when we want. We also benefit from a capitalistic system that supplies us with goods and services that enhance our standard of living and improve our overall quality of life.

I have also noticed an increase in social and political attacks against our elected officials when the Bible teaches in Romans 13 that we are to obey the laws of the land by submitting to and praying for our civic leaders, even when they do not share our political views or ideology.

We also do not use social media to degrade or humiliate the people we want to "pay back" for hurts we've perceived or experienced. God holds us accountable for our malevolence (whether done maliciously or in jest). Besides, we would not want someone to degrade or humiliate us even if they felt justified to do so.

We do not keep a record of past wrongs as some self-appointed vigilante. If all of us did this, there would be no one left standing since we are equal debtors. The Lord rightly says in John 8:7, "Let any one of you who is without sin be the first to throw a stone...."

We do not lash out with verbal or physical attacks against someone who cuts in front of us when we are standing in line or vehicular traffic. We extend grace to the other person as our equal who happens to be sharing a very brief "flash" of our space and time (in comparison to the vast eternity we have yet to live).

Our new lifestyle should apply to all areas of our daily, human interaction. In this way, we become expressions of Christ's prophetic role by filtering everything we think, say, and do through a Bible-based perspective. In other words, we are people of the Bible who abide by its principles. Although we may listen to secular experts, the Word of God is the lamp for our feet that lights our path every day (Psalm 119:105).

We also exhibit His priestly role by being the living, holy sacrifices that are always acceptable unto God. Here, we intentionally consecrate every area of our lives to God through daily obedience so that the Lord's perfect plan for others and us will always prevail. Jesus taught that to follow Him; we have to deny ourselves and take up our crosses—daily—without fail (Matthew 16:24).

Then we live out His kingly role through our responsible and accountable service to others. Here again, we express prudence and justice in all our dealings with others. Exploitation of children, euthanasia, abortion, violent assaults (even those in video games), salacious and degrading entertainment, etc., have no place where Christ's scepter of righteousness and eternal justice exists (Psalm 45:6).

We know the unrighteous shall not inherit the *Kingdom of God* and we are bought with a price and belong to Him exclusively (1 Corinthians 6:9, 20). Thus, we use our bodies to glorify God by loving, fearing, and doing all we can to please Him because it is the right and proper thing to do.

I believe the *Tree of Life* reflecting in us can heal the nations, as God promised in Revelation 22:2. Our understanding of who we are from God's perspective enables us to practice a pure religion that is Spirit-driven and undefiled before God and the world around us.

Notes

[1]See: Douglas, 349, and William L. Reese, "Simon Magus," *Dictionary of Philosophy and Religion: Eastern and Western Thought*, 8th ed., (Atlantic Highlands: Humanities Press, 1991) 530, and Kenneth Scott Latourette, *A History of Christianity: Beginnings to 1500*, rev. ed., vol. 1, (San Francisco: Harper, 1975) 460.

[2]See: Reese, "antinomianism," 18–19. For a full discussion on Simon Magus and the *Gnostic* threat, see: Latourette, 123–125, and Philip Schaff, *History of the Christian Church: Apostolic Christianity*, 3rd ed., vol. 1, (Grand Rapids: Eerdmans, 1985) 566–567.

[3]Gallagher, Steve. *At the Altar of Sexual Idolatry*, reprint, (Dry Ridge: Pure Life Ministries, 2007) 26.

[4]MacArthur, John F. *The Gospel According to Jesus*, rev. ed., (Grand Rapids: Zondervan, 1994) 182.

[5]See: Warren Baker and Eugene Carpenter, "Qados," in *The Complete Word Study Dictionary Old Testament*, (Chattanooga: AMG, 2003) 976–977.

[6]Bauer, Walter. "ἅγιος," *A Greek-English Lexicon of the New Testament and Other Early Christian Literature*, revised and edited by F. Wilbur Gingrich and Frederick W. Danker, 2nd ed. (Chicago: University of Chicago Press, 1979) 9–10.

[7]Christian counselors and other qualified professionals can help us recover when our ability to function safely and appropriately has been hindered by the emotional and/or physical trauma we have experienced or from the addictive-compulsive habits we may yet struggle to overcome.

[8]Unless it's specified in our job description, we should not spend company time reading our Bibles and proselytizing other employees. The company's employee handbook may be a source for appropriate guidance here.

About the Author

Floyd Bland has given a life of Christian service as a pastor, teacher, and administrator. As the Executive Director for Not Of The World Ministries, Inc., he shares practical, Bible-based models for Christian living designed to help strengthen our Christian walk with God and others. His other works include *The Christian Heritage: God's Answers for a Searching World,* and *Radical Forgiveness Through the Eyes of Jesus.* Floyd is married to his best friend and helpmate. Together they have two grown children and a grandson.

www.ingramcontent.com/pod-product-compliance
Lightning Source LLC
Chambersburg PA
CBHW050437010526
44118CB00013B/1564